SIMON CALLOW is an actor, director and writer. He has appeared on the stage and in many films, including the hugely popular *Four Weddings and a Funeral*. Callow's books include *Being An Actor*, *Shooting the Actor*, a highly acclaimed biography of Charles Laughton, a multi-volume biography of Orson Welles and *Love is Where it Falls*, an account of his friendship with the great play agent, Peggy Ramsay. He has also written *Charles Dickens and the Great Theatre of the World*, published for the writer's bicentenary. Renowned for a series of one-man shows including *The Importance of Being Oscar*, *The Mystery of Charles Dickens* and *Being Shakespeare*, he wrote and starred in *Inside Wagner's Head*, which provided the inspiration for this book.

'Simon Callow has done operagoers a service by writing a short, funny book about Wagner ... An ideal introduction ... Mr Callow truly inhabits the personality of this extraordinary man, presenting him as a gargantuan figure: an ineffable genius who was also a monstrous grotesque of Balzacian proportions'   *Country Life*

BY THE SAME AUTHOR

Being an Actor

Acting in Restoration Comedy

Orson Welles, Volume 1: The Road to Xanadu

Charles Laughton: A Difficult Actor

The Night of the Hunter (BFI Film Classics)

Dickens' Christmas: A Victorian Celebration

Shooting the Actor

Orson Welles, Volume 2: Hello Americans

Love is Where it Falls

Charles Dickens and the Great Theatre of the World

Orson Welles, Volume 3: One Man Band

SIMON CALLOW

BEING WAGNER

The Triumph of the Will

WILLIAM
COLLINS

William Collins
An imprint of HarperCollins*Publishers*
1 London Bridge Street
London SE1 9GF
www.WilliamCollinsBooks.com

First published in Great Britain by William Collins in 2017
This William Collins paperback edition published in 2018

1

Copyright © 2017 Simon Callow

A catalogue record for this book is
available from the British Library

ISBN 978-0-00-810571-6

Printed and bound in Great Britain by
CPI Group (UK) Ltd, Croydon, CR0 4YY

MIX
Paper from
responsible sources
FSC
www.fsc.org
FSC C007454

This book is produced from independently certified FSC paper
to ensure responsible forest management

For more information visit: www.harpercollins.co.uk/green

To David Hare,
friend, adviser, beacon.

'Only those friends, however, who feel an interest in the Man within the Artist, are capable of understanding him.'

Richard Wagner,
A Communication to My Friends, 1851

CONTENTS

FOREWORD

In the summer of 2012, Kasper Holten, then artistic director of the Royal Opera House in London, asked me to create a show to celebrate the Wagner bicentenary. I threw myself at the vast literature, and emerged astounded at what I had found. I knew his work very well – had been a Wagnerian since early adolescence, knew all about *leitmotive* and the *Tristan* chord – but, apart from his notorious anti-Semitism, knew remarkably little about the man, his vast intellectual scope, his rascally sex life, his revolutionary politics, his heroic struggle to create Bayreuth. In particular, I knew nothing about his quite extraordinary personality. I determined to put what I had discovered into the one-man show I was evolving, with the result that the text that I read out on the first day of rehearsals lasted four hours. People came and went, had lunch, returned, and came back to find me still droning on. I couldn't bear to leave anything out. The moment we started rehearsing, of course, pretty well the whole of that text was jettisoned. With light, images, props and above all with music to evoke the man and his world, I pared it down and down. The first preview still lasted two and a half hours; I cut an hour from it overnight. The show we finally evolved – *Inside Wagner's Head*, I called it – gave, I think, a pretty fair impression of the furor he generated, both in himself and in other people.

The play tried to answer the question of what it was about him that creates such violent emotions, even today, two hundred years after his birth. When I was working on it, I bumped into a friend, an eminent, an internationally famous, musician, and told him what I was doing. 'Why??' he protested. 'Dreadful music. Dreadful man.' This book asks the same question, but in a different way and from another perspective. It offers a sustained though not, of course, comprehensive examination of how this diminutive and often rebarbative man, with only the sketchiest of formal musical training, imposed his work and his view of life on the world. In unflagging pursuit of his goal, he was titanic, demiurgic, superhuman – and also frankly, more than a little alarming. No one was ever neutral about him. His personality was so extreme, so unfettered, that he struck many people as teetering on the edge of sanity, both in the way he behaved and in the intemperate demands he made of them. He had, said Liszt: 'A great and overwhelming nature, a sort of Vesuvius, which, when it is in eruption, scatters sheaves of fire and at the same time bunches of roses and elder'. Volcanic imagery abounds in recollections of him: 'the little man with the enormous head, long body and short legs,' wrote the painter Friedrich Pecht, 'resembled a volcano spewing out fire and sweeping all before him … his true element was the most violent excitement'. Half-admiringly, Liszt described Wagner's ability to work his way round a room, systematically alienating everyone in it. 'It is his habit to look down on people from the heights, even on those who are eager to show themselves submissive to him. He decidedly has the style and the ways of a ruler, and he has no consideration for anyone, or at least only the most obvious.'

Many people ran a mile from him. But quite as many were hypnotised by him, eager to catch the bunches of roses and elder that accompanied the lava. However, they approached him closely at their peril. He sometimes had an annihilating effect on those who were drawn to him. 'I am,' he remarked to Cosima, 'energy personified.' He invited the composer Peter

Cornelius, part of his circle of young admirers, to stay with him and write music, but he laid out his terms in advance: 'Either you accept my invitation and settle yourself immediately for your whole life in the same house with me,' wrote Wagner, 'or you disdain me, and expressly abjure all desire to unite yourself with me. In the latter case, I abjure you also, root and branch and never admit you again in any way into my life.' Cornelius refused Wagner's generous offer. 'I should not write a note,' he told a friend. 'I should be no more than a piece of spiritual furniture to him.' It sometimes seems as if Wagner were exaggerating his own ogreishness for comic effect, but if so, the joke was rarely perceived as such, and it often turned nasty. He was quite capable of being amusing, jovial, even, when he was in the mood. He was surprisingly capable of sending himself up. But even on such occasions, he could turn in an instant, suddenly spreading terror where mirth had been before.

This temperamental excess was not a case, as in Peter Shaffer's presentation of Mozart, of a contradiction between the man and the artist: in Wagner they were one, as he insisted again and again. His temperament and the circumstances of his upbringing gave him access to parts of his psyche that most people – most nice people – put away from themselves. When he wrote music, it was his subconscious, with which he was on such familiar terms, that he sought to express. He went straight to the archetype, and he went in deep. Though his music contains ideas, it deals not just with the ineffable, but with the unspeakable. It unearths what has been buried within us. And some people found it intolerable, right from the moment his true voice as a composer was heard. Critics felt assailed by it, to an uncommon degree. A famous cartoon published in Paris in 1861 when *Tannhäuser* was first performed there shows a demonic, bug-eyed Wagner climbing inside a huge ear, armed with a hammer and driving a nail through the eardrum, as blood spurts out in all directions. His music was, many critics thought, right from the beginning, in some way unhealthy. Eduard Hanslick dismissed the music of the composer's highly original spiritual odyssey *Lohengrin* as 'mawkish, spineless and often affected: it is like the white magnesium light into which it is not possible to gaze for long without hurting one's eyes'.

Some people took it even worse: in a letter to his friend Edvard Grieg, the Norwegian poet Bjørnstjerne Bjørnson wrote of *Tristan and Isolde* that it was 'the most enormous depravity I have ever seen or heard, but in its own crazy way it is so overwhelming that one is deadened by it, as by a drug'. He found the plot to be immoral, he continued, 'but even worse is this seasick music that destroys all sense of structure in its quest for tonal colour. In the end one just becomes a gob of slime on an ocean shore, something ejaculated by that masturbating pig in an opiate frenzy'. When Wagner published the libretto of his gargantuan epic *The Ring of the Nibelung*, before he had written a note of the score, it provoked the pioneer psychiatrist Theodor Puschmann to publish a pamphlet called *Richard Wagner: A Psychiatric Study*, which roundly described its subject as a monomaniac and a psychopath. Nietzsche, too, after succumbing for a while to extreme Wagnolatry, turned violently away from him, proclaiming that Wagner was not a composer at all, comparing him unfavourably to Bizet. Recently, the British composer Thomas Adès described Wagner's music as a fungus. 'It's a sort of unnatural growth. It's parasitic in a sense – on its models, on its material. His material doesn't grow symphonically – it doesn't grow through a musical logic – it grows parasitically. It has a laboratory atmosphere.' By contrast, Baudelaire said, after hearing the overture to *Tannhäuser* for the first time, that the music expressed 'all that lies most deeply hidden in the heart of man'.

This was something quite new. Or maybe something very old. Something like Dionysiac possession, perhaps. From the beginning, Wagner got under people's skin. He didn't care whether his music gave formal satisfaction, or whether it struck people as being beautiful or exciting or dramatic. He was trying to bypass the audience's analytical brain. His aim was the unconscious, the emotional underbelly, the murky depths of human experience. Feelings were what interested him, he said, not understanding. So it's hardly surprising that Wagner's music bothers people. It was meant to. It's what he set out to do. He wanted to overwhelm his audiences – literally, to knock them off centre. He was a man without boundaries, and he wanted his audience's boundaries to overflow too.

No wonder that the theatre was where he found himself. The theatre was, indeed, at his very core. He came from a theatrical background: his stepfather was an actor, as were several of his brothers and sisters. He wrote plays from an early age, he staged shows in his model theatre, he gave highly charged recitations. All his life, he acted, joyously giving himself over to amateur theatricals and giving electrifying performances of his own librettos. As with Charles Dickens, it was said of him by shrewd judges that had he chosen to make a living in the theatre, he would have been the greatest actor of his time. There are similarities between the two men. Like Wagner, Dickens created epics from his imagination by sheer willpower, epics teeming with archetypal figures; both men were given to great treks up mountains and down valleys; both of them had an uncanny relationship to animals. These parallels only go so far; the contrasts between them are sharp, but in their way, equally illuminating – Dickens with his essentially comic vision, Wagner with his tragic view of life; Dickens's art at heart carnival, Wagner's profoundly hieratic; Dickens deeply in touch with his inner child, Wagner directly connected to his inner infant.

The book I have tried to write aims to give a sense of what it was like to be near that demanding, tempestuous, haughty, playful, prodigiously productive figure, but also to place him in his world. Wagner belongs as much to the history of ideas and indeed to the history of the nineteenth century as he does to the history of music. I am not a musician, either as performer or as musicologist. I am a well-informed music lover, but it would be entirely inappropriate for me to attempt musical analysis. All I can write about is the effect of the music. I am slightly comforted by the fact that this is the only way Wagner ever wrote about music. You will search his copious writings in vain for an analysis of his highly idiosyncratic and complex compositional practice. This originality of procedure is a vital part of what makes him extraordinary, and I have noted the evolution of his musical means. But what has fascinated me above all has been how Wagner served his talent, his exceptional loyalty to it, however rackety a life he might have been leading, however much pressure there might have been to betray it, however hopeless his situation might have seemed. Wagner is in some senses an unlikely hero, but his custodianship of his gifts, despite the reverses of fortune and the vagaries of his temperament, counts as heroic and inspiring, while his personality in all its extremity belongs to one of the most fascinating of all the occupants of the human zoo.

* * *

Wagner has been written about at greater length than any other composer. Superb books, some short and some hernia-inducingly long, have covered him from every possible angle; primarily interested as I am in how he lived his life day-to-day, my main source has been his own words, in his copious published writings and especially, perhaps, in the letters, great tracts of which have been translated into English. Above all, I found that my most sustained sense of the man came from a book I had somewhat dreaded reading – his two-volume autobiography, *My Life*, published privately from 1870 to 1880. In the event, it turned out to be as vivacious and candid as the greatest artists' autobiographies, every bit as compelling and stimulating as Benvenuto Cellini's or Berlioz's – and about as reliable. The circumstances of the book's writing (dictated to his then mistress, Cosima von Bülow, at the behest of his besotted patron Ludwig II, edited and brought to press by an equally – at that stage – doting Nietzsche) mean that its truth is rarely pure and never simple, but it leaps off the page. At the very least, it tells us how he wanted to be seen by the world, which was by no means as a plaster saint. It is the work of a master dramatist, which is how he saw himself.

VORSPIEL

On 26 August 1876, as the last notes of the first performance of *The Twilight of the Gods* died away in the newly built Festspielhaus, in the tiny Bavarian town of Bayreuth, 2,000 people sat shaken, inspired, enchanted – or appalled. Among them were the musical aristocracy of Europe: Liszt, Saint-Saëns, Tchaikovsky, Anton Rubinstein, Grieg and Bruckner, along with a good sprinkling of the actual aristocracy of Europe, two emperors, three kings, a handful of princes, two grand dukes. All of them, or almost all of them, were swept along on a cataclysm of emotion to equal anything that happened on stage that evening.

As the applause grew and grew, and before singers or conductor or designer or choreographer had appeared in front of the curtain to acknowledge it, a diminutive, stooping figure, familiar not just to the faithful but to the cultured world at large, the subject of a dozen photoshoots, two dozen portraits and a thousand cartoons, made his way somewhat lopsidedly to the front of the stage; his disproportionately huge head with its madly bulging eyes was topped by a floppy velvet cap set at a rakish angle. This man, this tiny man, sixty-three years old, but looking, Tchaikovsky thought, ancient and frail, was the hero of the hour, the sole architect of the vast four-day, fifteen-hour epic, every one of whose thousands and thousands of words and thousands and thousands of notes he had created, unleashing onto the vast stage gods and dwarves, dragons and songbirds, women warriors on horseback and maidens disporting themselves in the Rhine, digging deeply and unsettlingly into the subconscious, discharging in his audience emotions that were oceanic and engulfing – this man was the architect of all that; the architect, indeed, in all but name, of the very theatre in which the heaving, roaring audience sat. There he stood before them, the self-proclaimed Musician of the Future. He held a hand up, and in the ensuing silence, in the marked Saxon accent which he never made the slightest attempt to lose, he said: 'Now you've seen what I want to achieve in Art. And you've seen what my artists, what we, can achieve. If you want the same thing, we shall have an Art.'

That was the way he spoke.

By we, he meant, of course, the German people. The first, the most important thing he had to say, was that the great work he had brought into existence was, above all else, German.

At a celebratory banquet the following night, after an interminable and obscure speech by a Reichstag deputy, the Hungarian politician Count Albert Apponyi leaped to his feet unannounced and said:

Brünnhilde – the new national art – lay asleep on a rock, surrounded by a great fire. The god Wotan had lit this fire, so that only the victorious and finest hero, a hero who knew no fear, would win her as his bride. Around the rock were mountains of ash and clinker – the cross-breeding of our own music with non-German elements. Along came a hero, the like of whom had never been seen before, Richard Wagner, who forged a weapon from the fragments of the sword of his fathers – the classical German masters – and with this sword he penetrated the fire, and with his kiss he awoke the sleeping Brünnhilde. 'Hail to you, victorious light!' she cried and with her we join our voices: 'Three cheers to our master, Richard Wagner! Hip hip! Hip hip! Hip hip!'

So that was it: Wagner was the hero of the newly unified German Reich, which had come into being just five years earlier, and his music was its music. Many people, including many Germans, felt very uncomfortable about this new Germany, and *The Ring of the Nibelung* seemed to embody, in its grandiosity, its self-celebrating Teutonic tub-thumping, its primitivism, everything that worried them about it. Wagner himself, after a brief and unsuccessful flirtation with the masters of the new establishment, was already somewhat unenamoured of their policies: to his immeasurable disgust, one of Reichskanzler Bismarck's first acts had been to give the vote to Jews. Wagner also, more surprisingly, loathed the new climate of militarism and imperialism. He withdrew back into the kingdom of art where he would always be absolute monarch, where his will would always prevail, where he could explore the depths and the heights of human experience – by which he meant, of course, his own experience.

None of this – Wagner's creation of a new national art, his acclaim as the greatest German artist of his times, the creation of his custom-built theatre – could possibly have been predicted at any point in the composer's life up to that point. It was, to be sure, exactly what he set out to do, almost to the letter. But there was nothing inevitable about it whatever. The massive solidity of his achievement grew out of and existed in the face of profound instability, both internal and external, an instability which characterises every stage and every phase of his life and which indeed is at the very heart of his music. At every turn of the way, his vision, and he was nothing if not visionary, was in danger of being sabotaged, either by circumstances, or by other people, or – more often than not – by himself.

We know all this because he told us. We know everything about this extraordinary man, everything, that is, except the most important thing: how he created his music. Because even he, the great motor-mouth, the obsessive self-analyst, was unable to explain that. But everything else, we know. Not just because of the memoirs, the reviews, the police records, the biographies, but because, in a way unusual in a musician – almost unknown, in fact – he was driven to communicate verbally, to explain himself in conversation, in letters, in speeches, in diaries, in pamphlets, in books. He wrote about art, music, theatre, history, politics, race, language, anthropology, myth, philosophy. Above all he wrote about himself. All this self-centredness was not simple egomania, though it was that too. It was how he engaged with his creativity.

Before he could compose a note he needed to articulate his position, to formulate his philosophy, to put himself in relation to the work and to the world – to dramatise himself as an artist, one might say. And for those who were susceptible, this torrent of words and this vision of himself was bewitching – positively hypnotic. For others (including some of his closest associates) it was unnerving, dangerous, overwhelming, almost life-threatening. His production of himself was inextinguishable. Many people tried to stop him, to suppress him, to silence him. Nothing but death could stem the flow. Where did it all come from? What was going on inside Wagner's head?

ONE

Young Richard

In 1813, when Wagner was born, the instability which is at the heart of his temperament and his work was the universal condition. Napoleon's plans for world dominion were unravelling, but not quickly, and not without massive fallout. A year after their humiliating defeat in Russia in 1812, in October 1813 the French, fielding an army of young untried soldiers, fought a savage battle almost literally on Wagner's doorstep, right in the centre of the city of Leipzig where he had been born, five months earlier, on 22 May, in a modest apartment over a pub in the Jewish district. Leipzig was the second city of the newly created kingdom of Saxony-Anhalt, one of the nearly forty sovereign states that constituted the hollow remnant of the Holy Roman Empire, itself the heir to the Western Roman Empire. Germany as such existed only as an idea. An increasingly potent idea, but an idea nonetheless. The Saxons were Napoleon's allies, and along with the French they were brutally crushed in October 1813 by the brilliantly organised coalition of Prussian, Swedish, Austrian and Russian forces; during the battle – the biggest engagement in military history before the First World War – Napoleon's armies were in and around the city, fighting and losing the heaviest pitched battle of the entire interminable war. Over the three days of the battle there were 100,000 losses, near enough: 45,000 French, 54,000 allies; just disposing of the corpses was a huge undertaking, and rotting bodies were still visible six months after the cessation of hostilities. The citizens were in a state of abject terror. The world seemed to be falling apart: and it was.

1

Nothing would be the same again. Wagner claimed that his father, Carl Friedrich Wagner, a clerk in the police service, died during the hostilities as a result of the stress – that, and the nervous fever which had seized the city.

Richard, no stranger himself to nervous fever, of both the physical and the creative variety, was the ninth and last of the Wagners' children. He was baptised in St Thomas's church, the very church where Johann Sebastian Bach, in the previous century, had served as cantor for twenty-five years. This omen was not followed any time soon by evidence of musical gifts in the child; indeed, as a little boy Richard's inclination and talent were all for the theatre, no doubt because his mother's new husband, Ludwig Geyer, a family friend, was an actor. Wagner's mother Johanna had remarried just nine months after her first husband's death; young Richard was given his stepfather's name and was accordingly known for his first fourteen years as Richard Geyer. Some fifty years later, Wagner came upon passionate letters from Geyer written to Johanna while her first husband was still alive; it was clear from them that she and Geyer were already lovers. So whose son was he? The police clerk's, or the actor's? Who was he? Like more than one of his characters, he could never be entirely sure, but it was Ludwig Geyer's portrait he carried around with him to the day he died – not Carl Friedrich Wagner's.

After the marriage, the newly-weds moved, with the children, to the Saxon capital, Dresden, where Geyer was a member of the royal theatre company. Little Richard's new life was highly agreeable to him: Geyer, a deft and successful portrait painter as well as an actor, was a kind, funny stepfather and the house was always aswarm with theatre people and musicians, among them Carl Maria von Weber. The great composer was music director of the Dresden opera, but also conductor of the theatre company, for whose productions he wrote incidental music. Wagner remembered him being in and out of the house all day long, hobbling around bandy-leg-ged, his huge spectacles on the end of his large nose and wear-ing a long, grey, old-fashioned coat like something out of one of Wagner's favourite E. T. A. Hoffmann stories. The boy was an insatiable reader, losing himself in the newly published fairy tales collected by Jacob and Wilhelm Grimm; though showing no gift for performing music, he was obsessed by it, listening spellbound to the military brass bands which paraded up and down the streets, tootling out good old German folk tunes. Best of all, he had easy access to the thea-tre, where he could play as long as he liked in the props shop and the wardrobe department; he had no skills as a painter, Geyer noted, but his imagination knew no bounds, and his stepfather encouraged it.

And then, quite suddenly, Geyer was gone, when Richard was just eight, struck down at the age of forty-two. Arriving at the deathbed, the boy was sent to the room next door by his sobbing mother and told to play something: he had had some elementary lessons in the little country school he attended, and obliged with 'Üb immer treu und Redlichkeit', a sober transformation of Papageno's playful ditty *'Ein mädchen oder Weibchen'* from *The Magic Flute*, with pious words to match:

> Use always fidelity and honesty
> Up to your cold grave;
> And stray not one inch
> From the ways of the Lord

Hearing the lad play the sombre little piece, Geyer murmured, as he slipped away, 'Is it possible the boy has some talent?'

Once Geyer was dead – the second father Wagner had lost – little thought was given to his dying question: her youngest son's musical abilities was low on the widow's list of prior-ities. The decent sum of money Geyer had left her soon ran out; Johanna took in lodgers, including, for a time, the distinguished composer and violinist Louis Spohr, so music was always in the air. In a household filled with musically gifted children, only Richard had shown no aptitude for performing it, as his mother helpfully informed Weber, in Richard's presence. In fact, apparently unnoticed by Johanna, he was utterly consumed by music. The sound of a brass band tuning up put him, he said, into a state of mystic excitement; the striking of fifths on the violins seemed to him like a greeting from the spirit world. Later he developed a crush on a young man who played the overture to Weber's new opera *Der Freischütz* on the piano. Whenever the hapless youth came to the house, Richard begged him to play it over and over and over again. At twelve, he finally persuaded his mother to let him have piano lessons, which he continued with only up to the point where he was able to bash out the *Freischütz* overture for himself. From then on he bashed out every score he could get his hands on; his skill at the piano never improved to the end of his days. All his performances – and he was a compulsive performer – were a triumph of feeling over technique and mind over fingers; the same effort of will and imagination somehow, fifty years later, enabled him to play and sing through the entire *Ring* cycle, evidently to overwhelming effect.

For a year after Geyer's death, to save money, young Richard had been shunted aimlessly around his relatives, from Eisleben to Leipzig and back again; en route he picked up the art of acrobatics, a skill he proudly displayed to the end of his life, manifesting startling flexibility in his late sixties. Back in Dresden at last, he was sent to the city's famous old grammar school, the Nicolaischule. Johanna was determined that he should be properly educated, desperate above all else that he should never become an actor. Three out of her nine children had done so, with some success, but to her the theatre was

4

beneath contempt, barely an art at all, certainly not to be compared with the poetry or the painting she so admired. Severe – Wagner said he could never once remember her having embraced him – and strongly pious, she was given to leading impromptu family prayer sessions from her bed, dispensing moral precepts to each of her children in turn. She was determined to make a serious young man out of Richard.

All in vain. He was a terrible student, lazy and wilful, refusing to study anything that failed to engage his imagination, which left exactly two subjects: history and literature – ancient Greek history and literature to be precise, with a bit of Shakespeare thrown in. His forte was recitation. At twelve, he made a big success speaking Hector's farewell from the *Iliad*, followed by 'To be or not to be' – in German, of course, both of them: languages, he said, were too much like hard work. Nevertheless, even in translation, Greek plays, Greek myths, and Greek history grabbed him by the throat from an early age. He wrote copiously himself, great poetic screeds, blood-spattered epics: it was the *gruesome*, he said, that aroused his keenest interest, invading his dreams, and giving him, night after night, shattering nightmares from which he would wake shrieking; understandably his brothers and sisters refused to sleep in the same room with him. He seems to have been, to put it mildly, a bit of a problem child. There may have been some anxiety – some uncertainty – in the air. There was very likely a sense in the household that Richard was Geyer's son. Nor did he fit in at school: a histrionic, hyperactive, oversensitive little chap with a nasty habit of bursting into tears every five minutes, but nonetheless he somehow managed to corral some of his school fellows into giving a performance (heavily abridged, one can only assume) of his favourite opera, Weber's *Der Freischütz*. In the opera a young man with ambitions to succeed the Head Forester and marry his daughter is outshot by a rival; frustrated, he turns to his saturnine colleague Kaspar, who gives him a magic bullet, promising to give him more if he will come with him to the Wolf's Ravine, which is where they go at the end of the second act.

In that famous scene, which terrified its first audiences and positively obsessed the young Wagner, the central characters, the hero Max and his darkly brooding friend Kaspar, repair at midnight to the fearsome ravine, deep in the woods. The clearing they are heading for is a vertiginously deep woodland glen, planted with pines and surrounded by high mountains, out of which a waterfall roars. The full moon shines wanly; in the foreground is a withered tree struck by lightning and decayed inside; it seems to glow with an unearthly lustre. On the gnarled branch of another tree sits a huge owl with fiery, circling eyes; on another perch crows and wood birds. Kaspar, in thrall to the devil, is laying out a circle of black boulders in the middle of which is a skull; a few paces away are a pair of torn-off eagle's wings, a casting ladle, and a bullet mould:

> Moonmilk fell on weeds!
> Uhui!

moans a chorus of Invisible Spirits,

> Spiders web is dewed with blood!
> Uhui!
> Ere the evening falls again –
> Uhui!
> Will the gentle bride be slain!
> Uhui!
> E're the next descent of night,
> Will the sacrifice be done!
> Uhui! Uhui!

In the distance, the clock strikes twelve. Kaspar completes the circle of stones, pulls his hunting knife out and plunges it into the skull. Then, raising the knife with the skull impaled on it, he turns round three times and calls out:

> Samiel! Samiel! Appear!
> By the wizard's cranium,
> Samiel, Samiel, appear!

Samiel appears. Kaspar, who has already sold his soul to this woodland devil, tries to do a deal with it: Samiel can have Max instead of him. The Spirit agrees; Max, knowing nothing of this, arrives and together – in spite of a scary warning from his mother's ghost, which suddenly looms up – he and Kaspar cast seven magic bullets, six of which will find their mark, the seventh will go wherever Samiel decrees. Finally, at the very last moment, and thanks to the intervention of an ancient hermit, the seventh bullet, instead of killing Max, finds its way into Kaspar's heart. Max is redeemed, and is free to marry his beloved Agathe.

Despite the redemptive ending this is gruesome stuff, all right, and strangely disturbing. The old story stirs up memories of a pagan German past, of nomadic warriors who come from the dark and terrible forest, where, in the grip of demonic powers, they commune with spirits. Weber tapped into all of that, creating German Romantic opera at a stroke, and scaring the pants off his audiences, not least sixteen-year-old Richard Wagner; its atmosphere, and its music, entered into his soul.

Meanwhile his flagrant neglect of his schoolwork finally forced a crisis, which he precipitated by disclosing to his family that he had written a play, *Leubald and Adelaïde*, loosely based, he said, on *Hamlet*, *King Lear*, *Richard III* and *Macbeth*, with a few bits of Goethe's *Götz von Berlichingen* thrown in for good measure. It was essentially *Hamlet*, he said, with the interesting difference that the hero, visited by the ghost of his murdered father, is driven to acts of homicidal revenge and goes mad – really mad, unlike Hamlet: in a frenzy, he stabs his girlfriend to death then, in a final blood-drenched tableau, he kills himself. The total roll call of the dead by the end of the play is forty-two. Or so Wagner said. In fact, as the recently rediscovered text reveals, it was no more than twelve, which tells us that Wagner was not averse to sending up his youthful self.

Whether it was twelve corpses or forty-two, the family were horrified to think what dark and desperate thoughts, how much violence and death, were swirling around inside the sixteen-year-old's brain. Not least disturbing among the play's catalogue of murders, rape and incestuous love – Adelaide is Leubald's half-sister – is the prominence given to the *Hamlet*-like murder of Leubald's father by his own brother; he then swiftly marries the widow, which might have seemed rather close to home for Johanna Wagner. All through the outraged tirades which rained down on his head, Wagner was laughing inwardly, he said, because they didn't know what he knew: that his work could only be rightly judged when set to music, music which he himself would write – was indeed about to start composing immediately. The fact that he had no idea how to go about such a thing was a minor obstacle. Under his own steam, he found a fee-paying music lending library and took out Johann Bernhard Logier's elementary compositional handbook, *Method of Thorough-bass*. He kept it so long, study-ing it so intently, that the fees accumulated alarmingly; the words 'borrow' and 'own' were always interchangeable in Wagner's mind. This particular music lending library was, as it happens, run by the implacable Friedrich Wieck, whose daughter Clara was before very long about to defy him by marrying Robert Schumann; Wagner failed to deflect him, and so, at the age of sixteen, he found himself being pursued for debt, an experience with which he would become all too familiar. His family was eventually called on to bail him out; that too was a pattern that became wearyingly familiar.

His family's dismay at having to pay was matched by their horror at discovering the nature of Richard's musical ambitions: to be an aspiring performer is one thing – at least there is a chance of earning a living. But to want to be a composer is quite another thing, a recipe for penury. He was not to be gainsaid: the willpower that was to drive his life forward was already fully formed: he was going to be a composer. Faced with the inevitable, the family procured him lessons in harmony (which bored him) and in violin (which tortured them), but neither the boredom nor the torture lasted very long: no sooner were both begun than they were abandoned. He went his own way; for him it was the only way possible. What really mattered to him was cultivating his imagination. He immersed himself in the writing of that phenomenal figure Ernst Theodor Amadeus Hoffmann – critic, composer, storyteller, journalist, embodiment and avatar of everything that was dark and fantastical in German Romanticism. Above all for the young Wagner, Hoffmann was the creator of the misunderstood musical genius Johannes Kreisler, rejected by society but certain of his own greatness; for Kreisler music is nothing less than a form of possession:

Unable to utter a word, Kreisler seated himself at the grand piano and struck the first chords of the duet as if dazed and confused by some strange intoxication … in the greatest agitation of mind, with an ardour which, in performance, was certain to enrapture anyone to whom Heaven had granted an even passable ear … soon both voices rose on the waves of the song like shimmering swans, now aspiring to rise aloft, to the radiant, golden clouds with the beat of rushing wings, now to sink dying in a sweet amorous embrace in the roaring currents of chords,

until deep sighs heralded the proximity of death, and with a
wild cry of pain the last *Addio* welled like a fount of blood from
the wounded breast.

Young Wagner gobbled up these stories, as well as devouring
Hoffmann's intensely imagined analyses of Beethoven's music
– less critical appreciation than Dionysiac trance.

> Beethoven's instrumental music unveils before us the realm of
> the mighty and the immeasurable. Here shining rays of light
> shoot through the darkness of night and we become aware of
> giant shadows swaying back and forth, moving ever closer
> around us and destroying *us* but not the pain of infinite yearn-
> ing, in which every desire, leaping up in sounds of exultation,
> sinks back and disappears. Only in this pain, in which love,
> hope and joy are consumed without being destroyed, which
> threatens to burst our hearts with a full-chorused cry of all the
> passions, do we live on as ecstatic visionaries

– which could easily be a description of Wagner's own mature
music. Intoxicated with all this, the seventeen-year-old
plunged in at the deep end, applying himself to the monumental task of making a piano transcription of Beethoven's
Ninth Symphony – a work written, in the view of most
contemporary musicians, when the composer was already half
mad. That was in itself enough to recommend it to Wagner.
Weber had remarked on hearing the first performance of the
Seventh Symphony that Beethoven was 'ripe for the
madhouse'; and the Ninth went further. It was the nineteenth
century's *Rite of Spring*, considered unplayable, incoherent,
crude, the *ne plus ultra* of all that was fantastic and incomprehensible. To Wagner it became, in his own words, 'the mystical
goal of all the strange thoughts and desires' he had concerning
music; the opening sustained fifths, he said, seemed to him to

be the spiritual keynote of his own life. Its darkness, its mystery, its implication of profound chaos, found an answering echo in his teenage soul, and never ceased to connect to him at the deepest level. He returned to this music again and again throughout his life; it was played at the opening of the first Bayreuth Festival and has been played at every opening since. It was, he felt, what music should be. What *his* music should be, though he had no idea how that might come to pass. The adolescent Wagner was almost morbidly susceptible to impressions; they overwhelmed his mind and his imagination, entering him like viruses, stirring up an inner furor, stoking his heightened sense of being, setting him on fire, mentally and physically. Encountering the Ninth Symphony of Beethoven was the overwhelming experience of his young manhood.

The next massive hit his system took, he said, was seeing the soprano Wilhelmine Schröder-Devrient in *Fidelio*, in the Leipzig theatre. Schröder-Devrient, then just twenty-eight, was the Maria Callas of her day: vocally unreliable, but expressively thrilling, every note, every word, every gesture deeply imbued with meaning. He despised the operatic performers he had seen up to that point: staring straight out at the audience, rooted to the spot, playing to the gallery, straining for stratospheric top notes. The vehicles in which they performed were equally beneath contempt; to the young Wagner, opera was a cartoon medium. But this was different. Every note, every word, every gesture meant something. The combination of Wilhelmine Schröder-Devrient and Beethoven convinced him that opera was the greatest form of human communication available. Forty years later he claimed that no event in his life produced so profound an impression upon him as seeing Schröder-Devrient on stage; he spoke about 'the almost satanic ardour' which the intensely human art of this incomparable actress (as he called her: actress, not singer) poured into his veins.

As it happens, it seems that Wagner could not have seen Shröder-Devrient sing Leonora. But to spur himself on, he linked his two gods together. Schröder-Devrient in whatever it was she sang knocked him sideways: the thought of Schröder-Devrient in Beethoven was tantamount to ecstasy. Having imagined it, it became real for him. That was the combination he sought in his work, for the rest of his life: sublime performance allied to supreme imagination.

He wrote her a passionate letter – of course he did! – telling her briefly (he *says*) that he now knew what he had to do with the rest of his life, and that if in the future she ever chanced to hear his name praised in the world of art, she must remember that she had, that evening, made him what he then swore it was his destiny to become. The great singer had revealed his mission to him. But what to do about it? He knew perfectly well that he was utterly incapable at that moment of producing anything worthy of her. Nor did he know how to go about learning to. He despised the bourgeois world around him; above all he despised the education system, which had rejected him and everything that interested him. What did it have to do with the dark beauty he lived with in his imagination? He dismissed it with contempt.

He was by now more or less semi-detached from his family. He had been chucked out of one school and walked out of another. He gave himself over to what he called the dissipations of raw manhood, the student life of his day. He wasn't a student, as it happens, but he plunged in regardless. If he had had access to drugs, he would certainly have funnelled them into his system; as it was he drank, he fornicated, he debauched, he partied in the taverns and the whorehouses. He hung out with dangerous, crazy people; he talked, talked, TALKED, about the subject of subjects: himself – and of course, art, inseparable notions in his mind. He was Rimbaud; he was Kurt Cobain; he was James Dean. His companions in debauchery turned out to be rather disappointing: he poured out his confidences, his dreams, his desires, his analyses of the world's ills without caring what effect they would have. His excitement in expressing his ideas was the only reward he received; when he turned to his listeners, expecting them to confide in him as he had done in them, it appeared that they had nothing to say. They just liked horsing around. In the midst of all the ragging and the rowdyism, surrounded by so-called friends, he found himself, he said, quite alone. But these adolescent activities were not just indulgences: they formed a protective hedge – a ring of magic fire, he might just as well have said – around what he called his 'inner life'. Instinctively he knew that this inner life had to grow to its natural strength in its own good time. Even at that early age, running in parallel to the recklessness, the debauchery, the over-exuberance, was a beady instinct for protecting his gift, his genius, and what fed it, even though at this stage it was, even to him, totally invisible.

Having been thrown out of school, he embarked on private tuition, paid for by his mother. He tried learning Classical Greek but gave up almost as soon as he started. Johanna's patience, and her money, were not limitless: she told him he had to find a job. His publisher brother-in-law offered him work as a proof-reader on a new edition of Karl Friedrich Becker's monumental *World History*; reading this was, Wagner said, his first real experience of education. For the first time he got a sense of the broad sweep of human history – just at the moment, as it happens, that it was passing through one of its periodic crises. Louis XVIII, the last of the Bourbons, fell in 1830; he was replaced by the so-called bourgeois king, Louis-Philippe, which provoked a wave of democratic solidarity across Europe, in particular across the thirty-nine member states of the fragile German Confederation. Kings, grand dukes, electors all felt the ground trembling under their feet.

Saxony felt especially vulnerable. The reactionary King Anton shrewdly invited his liberal nephew, Friedrich Augustus, to become co-regent; a constitution was established.

At eighteen, restless, volatile Wagner sided with change. He quickly knocked off a *Grand Overture* to celebrate the new order; in it he graphically depicted the darkness of oppression giving way to the joyful new dispensation, the latter represented by a theme unambiguously marked *Friedrich und Freiheit – Friedrich and Freedom* – which blazed forth in triumph at the end. It was not performed.

Meanwhile, despite the new liberal constitution, the revolutionary aspirations of the student body in Leipzig rumbled on; there was unrest, swiftly quelled by the arrest of a number of students. Wagner, still working in his brother-in-law's publishing house, attached himself to them, fell in with their protest marches, sang along with them as they bawled out the great student anthem 'Gaudeamus Igitur':

> Down with sadness, down with gloom,
> Down with all who hate us;
> Down with those who criticise,
> Look with envy in their eyes,
> Scoff, mock and berate us.

He joined their angry demands for the release of the arrested students, and was with them when they descended on the house of the magistrate who had ordered the arrest. Finding that the place had already been lightly trashed, they plunged in and finished the job off. Wagner was among the most uninhibited of the rioters, intoxicated, as he put it, by the students' unreasoning fury: he smashed and pillaged with the best of them, drawn into the vortex – his words – 'like a madman'. The frenzy only grew; he and his fellows moved across the town, slashing and burning. They weren't drunk; this was a self-generating rampage. All the latent violence that was in Wagner found an outlet. The formless resentments that had been germinating through his childhood and youth – his fatherlessness, his mother's narrow outlook, his hatred of authority, his frustration at having no proper channel for the expression of his artistic dreams and fantasies – erupted in rampant destruction as he threw his lot in with the student rioters.

These exploits were viewed indulgently by the city: it was just the young gentlemen letting off steam, people felt. But when the workers started rioting, there was universal outrage. Indeed, Wagner drily noted, the student body offered itself as temporary policemen, in which capacity, drunk and disorderly themselves, they imposed the rule of law, stopping travellers and inspecting their visas. How Wagner longed to be one of these lords of misrule. Soon enough, despite lacking the slightest qualifications, Wagner became an undergraduate of the University of Leipzig, not on the academic course, but as a student of music – just in time to realise his supreme aspiration: membership of the Saxonia fencing club. The moment he enrolled, he challenged as many people as he could to duels. None of these challenges materialised, which is just as well, since he knew nothing whatever about fencing. Instead he took up gambling, to which he soon became addicted. The more he lost, the more he gambled. Pale, sunken-eyed and haggard, like something out of Balzac or Dostoevsky, he lived only to gamble; finally, he stole his mother's savings and bet them, convinced that with a high enough stake he could make a large sum of money. Miraculously, this is what happened, and he returned his mother's savings to her, considerably richer. When he told her what he had done, she fainted. He experienced a moment of celestial benison: 'I felt as if God and His angels were standing by my side and whispering words of warning and consolation in my ears.'

From his earliest years, Wagner saw everything in his life as happening *sub specie aeternitatis*; destiny was always pulling the strings. Thus redeemed by divine intervention, he hurled himself into creative activity: his purpose was nothing less than to turn the world of music upside down. Among the first fruits of his inspiration was an overture in B-flat major. To ensure that it made its full revolutionary impact, he used different colours for the various instruments, drawing attention to the mystic meaning of his orchestration: strings were red, brass was black. If he had been able to get hold of any green ink, he said, he would have used that for the winds. Astonishingly, the young Leipzig conductor Heinrich Dorn agreed to programme the piece. During rehearsals Wagner was forced to acknowledge to himself that the technicolor scoring made no appreciable difference to the playing, and anxiously noted that the big effect he had planned, whereby after every four bar phrase there would be a loud thwack on the kettle-drum, simply did not work. The conductor, however, insisted it would be splendid. At the concert, the audience were enchanted by this wonderfully predictable effect. He heard them calculating its return; *dum dum, dum dum, dum dum, dum dum THWACK*, they would chant along with the music; seeing how unerringly accurate their calculations were, he suffered, he said, ten thousand torments, almost passing out with misery. The audience was delighted; it could have gone on forever as far as they were concerned. And then quite suddenly, the overture came to a halt, Wagner having disdained to provide it with anything as bourgeois an ending. A silence ensued. There were no exclamations of disapproval from the audience, no hissing, no comments, not even laughter: all he saw on their faces was intense astonishment at a peculiar occurrence, which impressed them, as it did him, like a horrible nightmare. He was then obliged to take his sister Ottilie, the only member of the family who had come to the concert, back home, through the puzzled crowd. The strange look the usher gave him on the way out haunted him ever afterwards, he said, and for a considerable time he avoided the stalls of the Leipzig theatre.

This event hastened his realisation that without skill, craft, or technique he would never write anything remotely worthy of Schröder-Devrient. The idea of actually attending the classes he'd enrolled in at the university was, of course, beneath consideration. Instead, he made his way to Bach's old church (where he had, after all, been baptised) and sought out the cantor, Theodor Weinlig, and asked him to take him on. Weinlig agreed – on one condition: that he would give up composing for six months. Wagner accepted the condition: for half a year he wrote nothing but fugues, day in and day out; he and Weinlig would engage in counterpoint duels. Under this highly practical tutelage, he finally began to get a feel, he said, for melody and vocal line. Once the six months were up, his self-denying ordinance was over, and music poured out of him: symphonies, overtures, marches, arias, sonatas – all entirely faceless. His Opus 1 was, in fact, a piano sonata; it is almost comically lacking in personality. For some years, Wagner would set his own highly original musical identity to one side; he would learn by imitating other people. Not a hint of experiment, nothing to mark his work out as his. That was how he taught himself, as he told the very young Hugo Wolf at the end of his life: by imitating other composers, often those whose music he despised. 'You can't be original straightaway,' he told Wolf.

In his first three operas, he systematically impersonated Marschner, Meyerbeer and, of all people, Donizetti. This is quite extraordinary. Because, like it or loathe it, Wagner's music is unmistakeably his. To eliminate all traces of personality from it must have taken a considerable effort of will.

PARIS

TWO

Out in the World

In a very short space of time Wagner wrote three overtures and a bonny, rather Schubertian Symphony in C. All of these decently crafted pieces were performed in Leipzig, and were well received; the symphony was played by the great and renowned Gewandhaus Orchestra. Now nineteen, and with a beard coming, he set to work sketching out the libretto of his first opera, *The Wedding*. It is heavily indebted to Hoffmann: a drama of the night, erupting with violent love, the betrayal of a best friend, sudden death and coffin-side revelations. The story was taken from Johann Gustav Gottlieb Büsching's pioneering account of chivalry in the Germany of the Middle Ages, and Wagner determined that his first venture into opera would avoid easy effects or operatic embellishments: he would write it, he said, in 'the blackest possible vein'. The story was almost as violent as that of *Leubald and Adelaïde*: a bride is powerfully attracted to a stranger whom she sees at her wedding procession; the frenzied man later climbs up into her bedroom; she struggles with the madman, hurling him down into the courtyard where every bone in his body is broken. At his funeral, the young woman throws herself at the coffin; she sinks, dying, onto his lifeless body. Love and death intertwined: Wagner started as he meant to go on.

The first person to whom he showed the libretto was his elder sister Rosalie. His various delinquencies had taken a terrible toll on his relationship with his family; Rosalie – ten years his senior – was the one through whom he hoped to repair it. He had an intense affection for her, revering her exquisite taste, her cultivated circle of acquaintance, her sweetness and depth of soul; a successful actress, she was also the chief breadwinner of the family – though, he casually remarks in his autobiography, she had no talent. He harboured the most powerful feelings for her, feelings, he said, which could vie with the noblest form of friendship between man and woman. 'I really am a spoilt child, because I fret every moment I am away from you!' he wrote to her. 'I hope, my Rosalie, that we two shall spend *much time* together in this world. Would you like that? ... You will always be my angel, my one and only Rosalie!' She had neither husband nor lover; Wagner made it his task to bring joy into her life, principally by making a name for himself. So when he handed her *The Wedding*, it was a present heavily burdened with hope and significance. She didn't like it. Couldn't he, she asked him, write something a little more conventional? Hearing this, Wagner there and then, in front of her very eyes, tore up the precious manuscript, declaring that he would write something that did please her.

He had not yet turned twenty, but the certainty, the intensity, the ruthlessness so characteristic of him are all fully present in this action. He was to offer further proof of his uncommon strength of mind when Rosalie later introduced him to the admired poet, critic and theatre director Heinrich Laube. Wagner was mightily impressed by the sardonic, Byronic young star; this impression was heightened by the glowing review Laube gave the young composer's Symphony in C. Not long after, Laube offered Wagner a libretto he had originally written for Giacomo Meyerbeer, then the most successful, most admired, opera composer of the age. Without a moment's hesitation, Wagner turned it down. With absolute confidence, the twenty-year-old boy rejected a libretto written by one of the most important *hommes de lettres* of the day. Wagner knew what a libretto needed to be, and he was pretty sure this was not it. Laube had not written a libretto at all, Wagner felt: he had written a chunk of poetry. As such, it was no use to him. He now began work on his next opera by writing the text himself, as he would henceforth do for everything he ever wrote. This one – *The Fairies*, specially designed to please Rosalie, and convince his family that he was not a dangerous revolutionary – would be set in the Fairy Kingdom, and be composed (with more than a nod towards Weber, whom he continued to revere) in the then popular High German Romantic manner of Heinrich Marschner, composer of the current smash hit *The Vampire*. Wagner cordially despised Marschner, but he wanted to find out how he did what he did. And if the piece turned out to be a smash hit, so much the better. His libretto was adapted from *The Serpent Lady*, a dramatic fable by the eighteenth-century Venetian playwright Carlo Gozzi most famous for the plays *The Stag King* and *Turandot*; he had been introduced to it by his scholarly uncle Adolf, his father's antiquarian brother, who had translated the play. Wagner's adaptation was loose: the title role is dropped in the opera and the names of the central characters are changed to Ada and Arindal, the bridal couple, as it happens, in *The Wedding*, which suggests that he had not utterly dismissed the earlier work from his mind. Ada is half-woman, half-fairy; Arindal a young mortal king who loves her. After overcoming a hundred obstacles of increasing impossibility, they marry and live happily ever after in Fairyland, not a resolution to be found in any other work of Wagner's. He was writing it for his family, after all.

Wagner had by now realised that as well as mastering the art of composition he needed to learn his craft in a practical context, so when he was offered a job as chorus master and general factotum at the opera house in the small Bavarian town of Würzburg he accepted it with alacrity, brushing the dust of Leipzig University off his feet without so much as a backward glance. He owed the job to the good offices of his eldest brother, Albert, who was a tenor in the company. The job in Würzburg was the beginning of a prolonged provincial apprenticeship in the course of which Wagner acquired a remarkable variety of compositional skills that in the fullness of time he would cunningly deploy in his own work. The bulk of the repertory at Würzburg consisted of bel canto operas, principally those of Bellini and Donizetti, and Wagner was immediately pitched into preparing the chorus for them; from time to time he was called on to orchestrate – sometimes even to compose – interpolated arias for the operas. He took the work seriously – he was there to learn, after all – but despite his new sense of responsibility and his growing ambition, his former wildness was still liable to break out: one afternoon in a beer garden, he found himself irresistibly drawn into a brawl, taking great pleasure in landing a vicious blow on a totally unknown man to whose face he had taken an instant dislike. It was in Würzburg that he first discovered his powers of seduction, triumphantly snatching a young woman away for a night of love while her hapless fiancé was playing the oboe in the band at a country wedding, for all the world as if he were Ibsen's Peer Gynt, a character – voluptuous, arrogant, fantastical, visionary – with whom he had much in common. Short, oddly disproportionate and prone to an unsightly skin condition, he had never thought of himself as good-looking, but in Würzburg he discovered that he had a certain charisma that women found attractive; he also learnt that he could impress his male companions with his flights of verbal bedazzlement – when, that is, he wasn't bewildering them. Ideas, opinions, impersonations, cascaded out of him, unless he was being moodily silent, which was frequently the case.

It was in Würzburg that he composed *The Fairies*. He brought the finished score home to Leipzig, where he sang and played it for the family, pounding away at the piano, belting out all the parts. His skills as an executant were so dismally lacking, he said, that it was only when he had worked himself, like Hoffmann's Kreisler, into a state of absolute ecstasy that it was possible for him to do justice to anything. Fortunately, a state of absolute ecstasy came very naturally to him. For the rest of his life, he performed his operas for friends and family, always at full tilt. This particular performance had a special intensity about it: the entire thing, and the piece itself, were for Rosalie. It was meant, he said, to provoke some sort of declaration of love from her, and she knew it. When it was over, she gave him a kiss; was it a kiss of real emotion, or just affectionate regard? He never knew, he said. As a result of his performance, she used her influence to secure him the promise of a production of the piece, in Leipzig, for the following year.

Back in Würzburg, unstimulated by his duties, he gave himself over to reading, which threw him into a state of more or less continuous intellectual turmoil, a condition which persisted to the day he died. Driven by the autodidact's desperate desire to catch up, he read greedily and indiscriminately, snatching at everything that came his way – history, philosophy, poetry, novels. Laube, whose libretto the very young Wagner had so airily rejected, was writing a sensational novel in three parts, *Young Europe*, which became a rallying cry for a new generation of Germans, sick of being weighed down by the burden of the past. Wagner devoured the book, along with the still-popular *Ardinghello*, Johann Jakob Wilhelm Heinse's sexually charged novel from thirty years earlier, which had contrasted the oppressive joylessness of German life with the voluptuous naturalness of the Mediterranean. Eagerly embracing the cause of free love and rejecting the tyranny of authority, Wagner determined to translate the literary revolution into a musical one and throw off the heaviness and tedium of German opera. He saw Schröder-Devrient again, this time in Bellini's Romeo and Juliet opera, *I Capuleti e i Montecchi*; the daring, romantic youthfulness of her Romeo, he said, drove him nearly mad with excitement – her performance made all the German operas he had seen (apart, of course, from *Fidelio*) seem feeble, stuffy, undramatic.

For the first, but by no means the last, time, Wagner took to print to express himself, in a little essay called 'On German Opera', in which he tore into the fairy opera *Euryanthe* by his former hero Weber:

> What splitting of hairs in the declamation, what fussy use of this or that instrument to emphasise a single word! Instead of throwing off a whole emotion with one bold freehand stroke, [Weber] minces the impression into little details and detailed littlenesses. How hard it comes to him, to give life to his Ensembles; how he drags the second Finale! And since the audience is bound to admit in the end that it hasn't understood a note of it, people have to find their consolation in dubbing it astoundingly *learned*, and therefore paying it a great respect. – O this wretched erudition – the source of every German ill!

He ends with a barely concealed self-advertisement:

> Only by a lighter and freer touch can we hope to shake off an incubus that has held our music by the throat, and especially our operatic music, for many a year. For why has no German opera-composer come to the front since so long? Because none knew how to gain the ear of the people – none has seized Life as it is: true and warm.

To put his new passion for Mediterranean art into effect, he immediately embarked on a new opera, based on Shakespeare – *Measure for Measure*, of all chilly, harsh plays, transposed to Sicily, with only one German character, based on Angelo,

Shakespeare's hypocritical Puritan: the governor, Friedrich, who epitomises the life-negating Teutonic world view. The play's complex and bitter working out of its themes he discarded: all twenty-one-year-old Richard Wagner was interested in was exposing the sinfulness, hypocrisy and unnaturalness of what in Germany passed for morality. His purpose was simple: to celebrate free love, lauding the sexy values of the south – sensuality, romance, passion. He called his opera *The Ban on Love* and this time when he wrote, he ripped off the gloomy mask of Marschner, pretending instead, remarkably convincingly, to be Donizetti or Bellini in their sunnier moments.

By the time he started writing *The Ban on Love* he had been offered a new job as chief conductor of the opera house in the once-splendid watering hole of Bad Lauchstädt in Saxony-Anhalt. Visiting the place for the first time, Wagner was dismayed by the dreariness and dowdiness of both the town and the theatre, once the stomping ground of Schiller and Goethe. In *My Life* he describes with grim relish the Dickensian scene that awaited him. The madly quirky director of the theatre introduced him to his gargantuan wife, who, crippled in one foot, lay on an enormous couch, while an elderly bass – her admirer – smoked his pipe beside her. The stage manager told Wagner that he would be expected to conduct *Don Giovanni* in two days' time; rehearsing it, he warned, might be difficult because of the intermittent availability of the town bandsmen, who formed the bulk of the orchestra. Appalled, Wagner made his excuses and was about to leave when he bumped into the company's exceedingly pretty leading actress, Fräulein Minna Planer. After a five-minute conversation with her, he changed his mind about going, and three days later, Wagner found himself leading the company, to some acclaim, in Mozart's most complex and demanding score; he had never conducted anything before in his life. The following night he was on the podium again for the latest Viennese musical comedy hit, that 'dust cloud of frivolity and vulgarity', as he called it, Nestroy's *Lumpazivagabundus*, in which Minna Planer played the Amorous Fairy, a role she was very soon to assume in his life.

The sexual pull between him and Minna was very strong, but what he was really after was a woman who had the qualities he lacked. At twenty-one, he was barely house-trained, arrogant, impetuous, outspoken. His face was often covered in ugly red blotches, lesions and pustules, the effects of the distressing dermatological condition erysipelas, otherwise known as Holy Fire, which at times of tension (or inspiration) erupted all over him from head to toe. He was still in the grip of a Bohemian contempt for anything bourgeois: on the road with the company he and his friend the poet Guido Apel had somehow managed after a boozy supper to reduce the huge, massively built Dutch tile-stove in their room to rubble. On the same tour he pitched into another riot, fists flying, with a few like-minded spirits, and for a while he took up gambling again. This prolonged adolescence, he realised, could not go on. Minna offered the stability he knew he needed. She was twenty-five, exceptionally pretty and completely unfazed by his facial blotches and swellings. Nor was she perturbed by his stone-age social demeanour; she could take it all in her stride. She was a natural homemaker, she was socially skilful, and, on some fairly slender evidence, she believed in him absolutely. She herself was not without emotional baggage: when she was fifteen she had had a child, Nathalie, from a liaison with a blackguardly aristocratic guardsman, who immediately dumped her and their daughter; the girl had been brought up believing that she was Minna's sister, not her daughter. Wagner was more than happy to accept this situation. For an apostle of free love, such trifles were neither here nor there. An effective operator and a brilliant diplomat, Minna eased his path in the theatre, introducing him to the people that mattered, making sure he was properly turned out, smoothing feathers he'd ruffled.

This was necessary because he was in a state of permanently boiling rage. Conducting a repertory which, by and large, he despised, was bad enough; but the impossible conditions backstage, the wretched quality of the singers, the comic inadequacy of the chorus and orchestra, all drove him to the brink, to say nothing of the fact that his Amorous Fairy was, at this early point in their relationship, by no means his alone. Minna and he broke up, temporarily, the first of many such ruptures; when they got together again, he told himself that what she felt for him was neither passion nor genuine love, nor was she capable of such a thing; her feeling for him, he decided, was one of heartfelt goodwill, sincere desire for his success, and genuine delight at and admiration for his talents. On that basis, they became an official couple, though the absence of passionate and fervent commitment rankled at subterranean levels. His account of his early relationship with Minna was admittedly dictated twenty years later to his then-mistress, for the gratification of his royal master, but his analysis is typical of the way his mind worked, ruthlessly weighing up the advantages and disadvantages of every situation in which he found himself. What did he need? And was he getting it?

The Leipzig theatre, meanwhile, reneged on the promise Rosalie had wrested from it to stage *The Fairies*. Wagner was unmoved by the cancellation. He conducted the evocative, Weber-like overture in Magdeburg, where the Lauchstädt company were wintering, and then promptly dismissed the rest of the opera from his mind, even banishing it from the catalogue of his works; it was not performed complete until five years after his death. It has hints throughout, both orchestrally and dramatically, of elements that Wagner would later develop. But simply having written it was enough for him. He had no further use for it: on, on. He threw himself into finishing *The Ban on Love*, and then helped out with incidental music for the local theatre. The overture he composed for *Columbus*, an historical drama written by his drinking companion Apel, shows his passion for innovative effects: he was attempting, he said, to depict both the ship and the ocean, simultaneously. Out of the orchestral commotion emerges what he called an 'exquisite, seductively dawning theme', representing a bewitching, chimerical vision, a Fata Morgana. This theme – suggesting the promised land towards which Columbus and his crew are speeding through choppy waters – is first stated by three pairs of trumpets each of a different pitch; after many adventurous modulations, the theme finally appears at the end of the piece triumphantly blazoned forth in the same key on all six trumpets: America in the sailors' sights as the sun rises over the ocean. To ensure maximum impact, he imported half a dozen trumpeters from the local barracks. The effect was, as intended, overwhelming, and completely upstaged the play, Wagner reports with some satisfaction.

He was heavily in debt, as he had been more or less continuously since leaving home – and even before. His idol, Wilhelmine Schröder-Devrient, who was passing through Magdeburg, generously offered to take part in a benefit for him. The programme was ambitious, and very, very noisy. In addition to Schröder-Devrient's contributions, there was his own *Columbus* overture, with its screaming trumpets, followed by Beethoven's brass-heavy *Victory Symphony*, which calls for alarming artillery effects. Expecting capacity business, he had hugely augmented the orchestra; the firing of the cannon and musketry in the Beethoven was organised with the utmost elaboration, by means of specially and expensively constructed apparatuses; trumpets and bugles, on both French and English sides, had been doubled and trebled. Alas, almost nobody came. The monstrously inflated orchestra, to say nothing of the volleys of ammunition, attacked the tiny audience with such overwhelming superiority of numbers that they swiftly gave up all thought of resistance and took flight. The net result was that he ended up infinitely worse in debt.

For want of any other work, and desperately in need of money, Wagner returned to Magdeburg the following season; on the way he stopped overnight in the medieval city of Nuremberg, where – somehow inevitably – he got caught up in a riot: it suddenly raged across the town, and equally suddenly dispersed, so that he and his brother-in-law were able to stroll arm in arm through the moonlit streets, quietly laughing; that, too, logged itself in his voluminous memory for future use, until, thirty years later, it turned up in Act II of *The Mastersingers of Nuremberg*. During his second season in Magdeburg he strengthened the repertory, the orchestra and the chorus, importing Prussian army singers and players. As a reward for all this, they let him put on the now-completed *Ban on Love* as a benefit. It's a busy, witty, bubbly, interminable score, drenched in southern sunshine. Rehearsals proceeded well enough, with Wagner inspiring the ill-prepared singers to some semblance of accuracy and lightness of touch, but when they actually started performing in the theatre, in front of an audience, vainly trying to keep abreast of the complex action and listen out for their musical cues, the whole thing collapsed into musical and dramatic mayhem. The revolutionary content of his opera, Wagner drily remarked, was lost on both authorities and audience, since what they saw on stage was completely unintelligible.

Inexplicably even to him, the reviews were deemed rather good, enough to warrant a second performance, but word of mouth had done its deadly work. He peered out into the auditorium and saw just two people in the stalls: his wealthy patroness, a certain Mme Gottschalk, and a Polish Jew dressed in full traditional garb. No one else. As Wagner made his way to the podium there was a piercing scream from behind the curtain: the prima donna's husband, believing that the very handsome second tenor had seduced her, had punched him in the face, which was now covered in blood. The prima donna noisily remonstrated with her husband, who then punched her too, at which point she went into convulsions. The rest of the company joined in, some on the husband's side, some on the wife's; at the end of this fracas, so many people were injured that the diminutive stage manager had to go before the curtain to announce that, due to circumstances beyond his control, the performance would not be taking place; the four people in the auditorium (two more had by then slipped into the circle) didn't seem to mind at all.

Thus Wagner's career in Magdeburg collapsed into farce. His hopes of a fortune from the benefit were dashed. His creditors nailed a summons to his door, and, as if in disgust, his brown poodle, which he loved deeply, ran away. The following day, looking out of the window of a friend's house, where they were hiding from the creditors, he and Minna saw a man fling himself into the river Elbe; then, a few days later, in accord with the odd aura of violence which always seemed to accompany him, Wagner found himself in a large and appreciative crowd witnessing the punishment of a soldier who had murdered his sweetheart. The luckless man was strapped to a wheel and crushed under it, breaking every bone in his body, which was then twisted, still breathing, through the spokes of the wheel.

Time, Wagner couldn't help feeling, to leave. Minna was already in far-off Königsberg, working in the theatre there; Wagner darkly suspected her of being involved with another man. He got there as fast as carriage could take him and proposed to her. She accepted, but as they hurtled towards matrimony, Wagner found the whole thing increasingly unreal. They fought furiously all the way to the church and continued in the sacristy until the pastor came in, at which point they pretended that everything was going marvellously; that sent them into fits of giggles, from which they found it difficult to recover as they entered the church. The congregation consisted entirely of actors and singers from the theatre, dressed up to the nines; there was not a single real friend among them. The heartless frivolity of the event chilled Wagner, he said. The pastor, at least, took it seriously – maybe rather too seriously, delivering a severe sermon in which he warned them of dark days ahead. There was, he said, a glimmer of hope: they would be helped by an unknown friend. Wagner perked up at this: who was this mysterious benefactor, he wanted to know. To his considerable disappointment, it turned out to be Jesus. During the wedding ceremony itself, he was so dazed that Minna had to nudge him to put his ring on the book. At that moment, he reports, he knew he had made a monumental mistake, and that his life was now divided into two currents: one faced the sun and carried him on like a dreamer; the other held his nature captive, prey to some nameless fear. He noted the exact time at which this thought came to him: 'It was eleven o'clock on the morning of the 24th November 1836 and I was twenty-three and a half years old.'

His forebodings were quickly confirmed. Neither as an artist nor as a woman was Minna his ideal, he knew that. She had no real talent for acting, and little interest in it; she was no Schröder-Devrient, not an artist, in any sense. All she wanted out of the theatre was to make a comfortable living. She had learned how to ingratiate herself with managements, deploying some fairly intense flirting, while keeping within the limits of respectability – just. She was physically attractive to Wagner, and her down-to-earth practicality and realism were useful. Her domesticity and comfortableness were the exact antipode of his own constantly striving nature and thus the perfect complement to him, but the temperamental gap jarred. In *My Life*, Wagner analyses all this with more than half a mind on the woman to whom he was dictating it, but it was very close to what he felt. His harsh analysis of Minna is typical of the way his brain worked, its maggoty, obsessive, unrelenting nature, even though the letters he and Minna sent each other tell a different story. 'Dear Minna,' he wrote a full seven years into their relationship, long past the first flush of lust, 'we absolutely ought never to be parted for long; that I feel afresh once more, both deeply and sincerely. What you are to me, a whole capital of 70,000 cannot replace.' She was not his muse; but he loved the sensual and domestic comforts she extended to him. For many years those comforts persuaded him to return to her; when they were together they often quarrelled; just as often, they experienced real companionship. But was companionship what a man like Wagner needed? In his analysis of Minna, he was, as so often, interrogating himself: what did he want from a woman? His relationship with them was always vexed. He seemed to be looking, not for a particular woman, but for women as archetypes, an unpromising basis for a relationship.

From the moment they were married, he and Minna fought; when they did, Wagner, it goes without saying, expressed himself with savage, vicious, brutal eloquence, making her weep bitterly; he would then apologise abjectly, treating her with an exaggerated tenderness, whose strained insincerity led to further and yet more savage outbursts; and so the cycle went on. After a year of this, Minna ran away, taking Nathalie with her. Wagner tracked Minna down to her parents' house in Dresden; they resumed their married life. Then she bolted a second time, this time in company with an admirer. Wagner went to live with his brother and sister-in-law, while he waited to take up a new appointment in the distant then-Russian city of Riga, hired to provide the sizeable German community there with the art of which they had been starved. Meanwhile he put all his emotional energy into his next opera, *Rienzi: the Last of the Tribunes*, drawn from the recently published run-away best-seller of the same name by Dickens's great friend Edward Bulwer-Lytton. The hero, a Coriolanus-like Roman tribune who is first acclaimed by the people, then despised and finally burnt to death by them, was the sort of man Wagner could readily identify with, but in reality he was drawn to the subject for one reason and one reason only: he thought it would give him a hit. He planned the opera, his third to be completed, on the grandest possible scale; disgusted with the inadequacy and parochialism of German provincial opera houses, he had no intention whatever of letting it be performed anywhere but on the largest stages in Europe. Giacomo Meyerbeer, the Andrew Lloyd Webber of grand opera, generating one smash hit after another, was his model; Paris, Meyerbeer's base, his destination.

He meanwhile set off for Riga, to open its grand and well-equipped new theatre. With the giant score of *Rienzi* more than half complete, he made the long and perilous journey to the Baltic. He was pleased with what he found. The Riga audience had sophisticated expectations of its opera, and were prepared to pay for it; Wagner was able to do much better work there than he had elsewhere. The theatre itself was distinctly state of the art, and he remembered its provisions when, much later, he came to create his own theatre. He was particularly struck by the simplicity of the auditorium, the orchestra pit in which the majority of the players were tucked under the stage, and the practice of lowering the lights in the theatre during the performance. In due course, a repentant and heartbroken Minna went back to him. She joined the local company, playing starring roles, and their domestic life resumed rather more happily than before. They were joined by Minna's sister, Amelia – a real sister, this time – and, for a brief period, a young wolf. Wagner was deeply fond of animals, and they of him; at various times he carted round a sort of domestic zoo, including hamsters and parrots. Throughout his life he was surrounded by dogs, the bigger the better. They were slavishly devoted to him, and fiercely protective. Wagner was fascinated by the wolf and tried to domesticate it; the creature proved untameable and was finally released back into the wild. After its departure, he acquired an enormous Newfoundland dog which he called Robber; he adored this animal, and the feeling was entirely mutual.

Wagner spent two long years in the snowbound, fogbound and rain-bound city. Despite his growing mastery over the orchestra, singers and chorus, the gap between what he was striving to create on stage and what his colleagues were either willing or able to achieve resulted in increasing agitation on his part. He now came to loathe what he disdainfully called 'theatre people'; he fell out with the director of the theatre and avoided all off-stage contact with his fellow artists. His greatest satisfaction came not in the opera house but from a sensational series of orchestral concerts he gave featuring music by Mozart, Beethoven, Weber and, occasionally, himself; fewer compromises needed to be made when singers and scenery were taken out of the equation. He applied himself vigorously and with detailed thought to the question of building up knowledgeable audiences – 'true lovers of art' – while also encouraging the merely curious. Everything must be done to ensure that the greater part of the audience regards the concerts as agreeable entertainment 'since we all know perfectly well that not every section of the audience has come to worship at the shrine of art'. A Swiss baker was engaged to take care of the buffet arrangements. The twenty-five-year-old conductor with his blazing ideals was also an entirely practical manager. His orchestra responded well to the demands that he made of them. 'We are giving so perfectly organised a body (as our orchestra may justifiably be described at present) an opportunity to show its strengths ... and to develop along independent lines; for what true musician would not be dismayed to be thinking of carrying out routine duties rather than achieving something that was genuinely enjoyable and edifying?' It was the opera house that was driving him mad. The truth is that he had had enough of provincial theatres; his heart was set on the greater world, and *Rienzi*, on which he had for many months been toiling, was to be his passport to it. He dreamed only of Paris.

His departure from Riga was abrupt, amidst the intrigues and vituperations so characteristic of him; Minna gave her final performance as Schiller's Mary Stuart, the proceeds of which enabled them to pay for their travel. Typically, Wagner was being energetically pursued by creditors, so in order to get past the Russian customs officers they needed to undertake an immensely complicated subterfuge, changing carriages and hiding in safe houses. The whole escapade took place under the beady eyes of heavily armed Cossacks. The roads were bumpy and dangerous. At one point, Minna was thrown out of the carriage; she later attributed her failure to conceive during their marriage to this incident. The journey, already quite dangerous and alarming enough, was rendered almost hallucinatory by Wagner's stubborn determination to travel with the dog, Robber, from whom at no cost would he be parted. The great shaggy beast sometimes loped alongside the carriage; sometimes they managed to bundle him into it. Life would be easier for the dog, they decided, if they were to abandon the carriage and complete the journey by sea, stopping at London en route for Paris, so they smuggled him on board, where he terrorised crew and passengers alike, taking up residence in front of the ship's grog, which thereupon became the exclusive preserve of the Wagners.

The crossing was, at first, becalmed, and then terrifyingly storm-tossed. Even the crew were unnerved, and began darkly to suspect that the Wagners and their dog had brought bad luck with them. Finally, after weathering these storms, the ship approached the English coast, whereupon the vessel ran aground on sandbanks. As they at last reached the mouth of the Thames, Wagner, despite Minna's bitter reproaches, fell into a deep and contented sleep, emerging from it shortly afterwards refreshed and full of energy. His powers of renewal remained prodigious to the end of his life.

THREE

Doldrums

London – the greatest city in the world, as Wagner called it – thrilled them. Even the traffic jams were impressive: it took the Wagners an hour to get from Tower Bridge to Old Compton Street, where they happily installed themselves with Robber, who then decided to do a bit of unilateral tourism – strolling back, two hours later, having had a good look at Oxford Street. The Wagners followed suit, doing some sightseeing themselves. Richard was trying to find the author of *Rienzi*, Baron Bulwer-Lytton, so, very sensibly, he went to the House of Lords; there he caught sight of the Duke of Wellington, and the prime minister Viscount Melbourne, but no sign of the celebrated author. He and Minna wandered the streets, surviving what Wagner calls the ghastly English Sunday, and took a train (their first ever) to Gravesend. Then, with Robber still at their side, they crossed the Channel by steamer, arriving at Boulogne, where they planned to stay for a few days. By remarkable coincidence, the man whose career Wagner intended to emulate – and then eclipse – was there. Giacomo Meyerbeer was, at the age of forty-eight, the most successful and influential composer in Europe, the toast of Paris (*Robert le Diable* and *Les Huguenots*, both global smash hits, had their premières there) and also the court Kapellmeister in Berlin. He inspired both the admiration and the envy of his colleagues, not only in the ambitiousness and scope of his work, but for his ability to turn composing into a profit-making concern: he was a shrewd businessman and a master of the arts of publicity, and he had the press neatly stitched up.

This was a man from whom a struggling young composer had much to learn, one way and another. During his time in Riga, Wagner had sent him a letter in which he told the great man that 'you can hardly rise to greater artistic fame, for you have already reached the most dazzling heights; you are almost a god on earth. I am not yet 24 years old,' he continued, cheerfully ditching his former god:

> I was born in Leipzig, and when I attended university there I decided to pursue a career in music. My passionate admiration of Beethoven impelled me to take that step, which explains why my first works were extremely one-sided. Since then, and since I have gained experience of life and of the musical profession, my views about the present state of music, particularly dramatic music, have changed considerably. Need I deny that it was your works, more than anything else, that showed me a quite new direction …

Understandably, Meyerbeer had not replied to this rhapsody. What would he have said? 'You're right. I am a god on earth'? Whatever his merits or demerits as composer or as a man, Meyerbeer had no delusions about himself. Having struggled to succeed, he was always willing to help out nascent talent: here in Boulogne, Wagner managed to get an appointment with him without much difficulty. He was impressed by the older composer. Meyerbeer's Jewishness did not escape his attention; stick in Wagner's craw though it might, it was no obstacle to his pursuit of him. 'The years had not yet given his features the flabby look which sooner or later mars most Jewish faces,' he said, graciously, 'and the fine formation of his brow round about the eyes gave him an expression of countenance that inspired confidence.'

Wagner brought the libretto of *Rienzi* to the meeting, along with the score of the two acts (out of five) that he had already completed. Meyerbeer listened attentively and with great courtesy to Wagner's spirited rendition of three acts of the libretto, and kept the score to study; in addition, he gave him letters of introduction to the manager of the Opéra in Paris and introduced him to his friends in Boulogne, including the great virtuoso Ignaz Moscheles, with whom Wagner spent some pleasant musical evenings. Wagner thanked Meyerbeer in language of some extravagance, bordering on the erotic. 'The gratitude I carry in my heart for you, my noble Protector, knows no bounds,' he wrote. 'I foresee that I shall be pursuing you, muttering my thanks, in this world and the next. I assure you that even in hell I shall be muttering it.' He signed himself off as 'your subject, forever bound to you, body and soul'. Later, when things hadn't moved forward as quickly as he might have hoped, he wrote: 'My head and my heart are no longer my own – they are already your property, my Master ... I realise that I shall have to be your slave in mind and body ... I shall be a faithful and honest slave.' This shameless effusion evidently worked. Even Wagner, who assumed that it was the responsibility of everyone he ever met to advance his career, was astounded at Meyerbeer's kindness. And of course he never forgave him for it. One of Meyerbeer's first and greatest successes had been *Robert le Diable*. Had he lived to see the wholesale destruction of his reputation and legacy that Wagner was to engineer, he might have reflected that in Boulogne, he had met Richard le Diable, his nemesis.

From Boulogne, the Wagners made for Paris, the epicentre of the operatic world. This was the old Paris of 1839, Louis Philippe's Paris: the Paris of a thousand little alleys and passages, before Napoleon III and his Prefect of the Seine, Georges-Eugène Haussmann, swept the old streets away. The Wagners stayed in an apartment in the house where Molière had been born, and soon formed a lively circle of acquaintance. Among them was Franz Liszt, whom he had met in

Berlin, just two years older than Wagner, but an international superstar, a pianist of superhuman brilliance, who was just beginning to compose music himself. Wagner was at first resentful of Liszt's celebrity status, but quickly acknowledged the charm, the originality, and the generosity of the man. He is the only individual of comparable power with whom he maintained a relationship that could in any way be described as an equal one.

But Wagner's Meyerbeer-brokered meeting at the Opéra came to nothing. He wrote a number of entirely conventional songs for various singers as calling cards; he managed to get a rehearsal of his *Columbus* overture, but not a performance. He and Minna lived from hand to mouth; so dire was their situation that when one day Wagner's faithful four-footed friend Robber loped off and never came back again they were actually relieved: it was one less mouth to feed. A little later Wagner's old associate, the poet-novelist-critic Laube, newly released from the Prussian jail in which he had been incarcerated for his inflammatory writings against the Saxon government, blew into town and managed to persuade a rich friend to provide the composer with a six-month stipend, which provided some relief. Nothing fundamentally shifted in Wagner's fortunes, however; he started to dream about going to live in America – in Maryland, about whose charms he entertained some imaginative notions. Money was again short. Still toiling over *Rienzi*, he started sketching a one-act curtain-raiser as a potboiler. He had come across his subject while browsing through the sardonic stories in Heine's collection *The Memoirs of Herr Schnabelewopski*, in one of which the hero sees a dramatised version of the old legend of the Flying Dutchman. As Wagner wrote, he found himself fiercely gripped by the material, which engaged him at a deep level; Heine, for whom the story is a mere backdrop to a seduction, concludes the episode with the words: 'The moral of the play is that women should never marry a Flying Dutchman, while we men may learn from it that through women one can go down and perish – under agreeable circumstances!' Wagner felt none of Heine's cynicism. He took the legend very seriously – and very personally – indeed. To him, the story of a man doomed to travel the world restlessly until he was redeemed by the love of a woman who entirely believes in him – who trusts him absolutely – stirred him profoundly. He wrote the libretto in a blaze of inspiration.

The libretto was speculative, a shot in the dark. He needed ready cash. In the absence of musical commissions, he eagerly accepted an invitation from Meyerbeer's friend and agent, Maurice Schlesinger, to write articles for his journal, the *Revue et Gazette musicale*. The tone of these pieces – unlike almost anything else in his vast literary output – is light and witty; accessible and provocative, they are excellent journalism showing him thinking sharply about the state of music in 1839, beginning to form an aesthetic, defining himself against other people. He writes about Italian composers, about his contemporaries Berlioz and Liszt, about the relationship between the public and the artist; he writes with intense feeling about Beethoven, and with great force about German music, whose future he clearly sees as being his responsibility; in 'On German Music', he is thinking out loud about his own needs and ambitions, trying to work out how he's going to take over the operatic baton from Mozart and Weber; the fairy-tale world of folkish innocence evoked by Mozart in *The Magic Flute* and Weber in *Oberon* does not seem to him to be the way forward. Though he was profoundly interested in what it was that made German music German, Wagner was no musical nationalist: not a single folk song appears in his music, or ever would. The distinctiveness of German music, he felt, was to be found elsewhere. He discusses these matters elegantly and pithily, but they are clearly of pressing importance to him in articulating his own position – in coming to an understanding of who he was and what he was trying to do. Wagner may be unique among composers, as Bryan Magee remarks, in his inability to write music unless he has clarified his own philosophical position. Here, in Paris, that process begins in earnest.

In one striking piece, the macabre story called 'Death in Paris', he writes about himself as if he were dead, which he must often have felt. It is a mordantly funny self-portrait, depicting a provincial German composer, 'R.', who mistakenly makes his way to Paris to seek his fortune, and includes a significant role for Robber, his fugitive Newfoundland dog. R passes through delusion and insanity until he ends up, starving and numb, on his deathbed in Montmartre, making a final statement which may well have represented Wagner's own deepest feelings:

I believe in God, Mozart and Beethoven, likewise in their disciples and apostles; I believe in the Holy Ghost and in the truth of the one and indivisible Art; I believe this Art to be an emanation of God that dwells in the hearts of all enlightened men; I believe that whoever has steeped himself in its holy joy must dedicate himself to it forever and can never deny it; I believe that all men are blessed through Art and that it is therefore permissible to die of hunger for its sake; I believe that in death I shall attain the highest bliss – that in my life on earth I was a dissonant chord, which death will resolve in glorious purity ... I believe in a Day of Judgement upon which all who dared to exploit this chaste and noble Art for the sake of profit, and all who in the baseness of their hearts dishonoured and disgraced it for the sake of sensual pleasure will be fearfully punished; I believe that they will be condemned to listen to their own music for all eternity. On the other hand I believe that the souls of Art's true disciples will be transfigured in a shining heavenly fabric of glorious harmony and be united therein forever – may such a lot be mine! Amen!

Like his alter ego R, he felt certain that if he could only achieve one drop-dead, knock-down mega-hit, he could then enter the kingdom of Art. *Rienzi* was to be that mega-hit. It was now at last – in all its vastness (three and three-quarter hours long, not counting intervals, of which there were four) – finished, replete with big fat tunes, huge public scenes, heroic arias and noisy ensembles in the manner of his 'noble Protector' Meyerbeer, on whose influence he continued to rely. His confidence in him was sorely tested the next time they met, when Meyerbeer helpfully suggested that Wagner should write a ballet, perhaps in collaboration with another composer, an idea – or rather two ideas, ballet and collaboration – which left Wagner speechless, an uncommon condition for him. While he was recovering from this affront, Meyerbeer recommended *Rienzi* to Dresden, an excellent suggestion, because the company had a tenor who could do justice to the massively demanding leading role. There was a problem, though: Wagner had no money to send the massive score to Dresden, so he set off around a heavily fogbound Paris trying to raise extended loans – in vain. A cheesemonger in the Cité was his last hope. Hurrying past the church of St Roch, guardian saint of plague victims – the statue of the saint on the outside of the church, his body covered in sores, his dog at his side – Wagner was startled to glimpse, peering through the dense fog which enveloped the city, his beloved Newfoundland, Robber, who had decamped months before. Clutching the large metronome he happened to have with him, Wagner gave the animal chase all over Paris, but finally it eluded him, never to return. It seemed a horrible omen to Wagner. The whole scene – the distracted, bug-eyed composer, the fog, St Roch, the Newfoundland dog, the cheesemonger, the metronome –

combine in a surreal image that in no way answers to the word Wagnerian, but *My Life* is full of such passages, suggesting a hallucinatory element in the composer's psyche which should by no means be discounted.

He finally raised the money and the score was sent. Life carried grimly on for the Wagners. He eked out some kind of a living by transcribing arias from the operas of Donizetti for piano, violin and cornet. No single fact can more vividly convey the depths to which he had descended. Occasionally he went to concerts. He was drawn to the music of Berlioz. *Roméo et Juliette*, *Symphonie fantastique* and *Harold en Italie*, all excited him, but it was the massive public lamentation of the *Symphonie funèbre et triomphale* for large military band and strings that shook him to the core; hearing Berlioz's work, he said, made him feel like a little schoolboy by comparison. Meanwhile, financial desperation bore inexorably down upon him and Minna. They moved out of the city into the suburbs, withdrawing from all society; he grew a full beard for the only time in his life. Fun was had sometimes in rare gatherings of friends, where he would give dazzling impersonations of the grotesque vocalisations so extravagantly applauded by canary-fanciers at the Opéra, but there was a bitter edge to the humour. Then, at long last, some luck, of sorts: he submitted his libretto for *The Flying Dutchman* to the director of the Opéra, who liked it, but wanted another composer, Pierre-Louis Dietsch, the theatre's chorus master, to write the music. Wagner gladly took the money: it bought him time to knock off the vocal score for his own opera to the same libretto in seven weeks.

And so it was that there in Paris, poor, desperate, angry, isolated – he could barely form a sentence in French – with three massive scores behind him, only one of which had been performed, and that only once, he wrote the first music which could only have been written by him. For the first time he had found a subject that stirred his deepest creative processes. And though the hero was Dutch, and the story set in Norway (eventually – it was Scotland to begin with), the music was unmistakeably German. And when he came to orchestrate it, he summoned up out of the orchestra pit a whole new world of sound. From now on that would be the way it happened for him. After writing the libretto – the poem, as he preferred to call it – he would wait for its atmosphere, its colour, its tonal flesh and blood to manifest itself. Sometimes it came quickly, sometimes it took years. With *The Flying Dutchman*, it surged up out of him; the terrible sea passage from Riga he and Minna had endured had already furnished him with the idea for the overture. The rest followed irresistibly and authentic-ally. After years of trying on other voices for size – Marschner, Donizetti, Meyerbeer – when he finally spoke with his own, it proved to be a profoundly stirring one.

There is nothing remotely anonymous about *The Flying Dutchman*; on the contrary, it is unmistakeably personal. The story of Vanderdecken, forced to roam the world until he finds redemption through love, obviously spoke to Wagner deeply: he could relate to that. But the figure of Senta, the woman prepared to give herself utterly and totally, up to and beyond the point of death, drew from him an act of intense imagina-tive identification. Wagner is both Vanderdecken and Senta; the redeemer and the redeemed. From now on the idea of redemption – through love, through sex, through God, through art – underpinned everything he ever wrote, with himself in it, right at the thick of things. He is both the one who needs redemption and the redeemer. What had he done that was so bad? And what qualified him to redeem, not just himself, but the nation, perhaps the world? Whatever it was, it was a destiny he embraced, the destiny, as he saw it, of the artist. The artist is he who suffers on behalf of humanity, and whose work is the cure for its ailments. Art was the only hope for mankind. It should therefore be at the centre of society. And at the centre of art was the artist. That was the logic that kept him going.

In the real world of Paris 1841, he and Minna, very far from the centre of society, eked out what was left of the money from the sale of the libretto. It was not enough to pay for shoe repairs: for a while, Wagner's boots had no soles. They were always, always hungry.

More pressing even than physical hunger, his desperation for intellectual nourishment drove him to read the subjects he had neglected at school: history and philosophy. His interest in these matters was not academic. He was looking for something: himself. The humiliations Paris had heaped on his head, and the contempt he felt for what Paris admired, led him to dig back into his roots, to reaffirm his identity and to delve into what he now recognised as the underlying source of all his artistic energies – his Germanness. Reverting to his youthful description of himself as a dramatist, he started writing a play, *The Saracen*, based on the life of the Holy Roman Emperor Friedrich II, that universal man – King of Germany, of Sicily, and of Jerusalem – who seemed to Wagner to embody the German mind and what he called its capacity to encompass purely human qualities, beyond the narrow bounds of nationality. This capacity he likened to that of the Greek mind, the ultimate praise from the young Wagner. The central relationship in the play, though, was between the emperor's lovechild, Fatima, 'the fruit of the embraces of Friedrich and a daughter of Araby', as Wagner put it, 'during a peaceful stay in Palestine', and his legitimate son and heir, Manfred, King of Sicily. Fatima is revered as a prophetess; when she and Manfred encounter each other, they experience an immense but unconsummated sexual charge. At the end of the play, she deflects a sword intended for him into her own breast. Wagner was nothing if not constant in his preoccupations – the erotic prophetess, sibling passion, impossible love, selfless salvation – but his vision of a multilingual, multicultural German world order belongs to the mindset that produced *The Ban on Love*, with its embrace of Mediterranean values.

He abandoned the play when he hit on another subject which was altogether closer to home, expressing both the German spirit and his own personal preoccupations: most particularly the eternal struggle between sensuality and spirituality. In Ludwig Bechstein's collection of medieval tales of Thuringian knights, he came across an account of the mythical court of the goddess Venus located on Hörselberg (otherwise known as Venusberg, the hill of Venus) between the towns of Gotha and Eisenach; he was fascinated by Bechstein's description of the minstrels' contest on the Wartburg, which he connected with the medieval legend of Tannhäuser, the thirteenth-century minstrel torn between the carnal delights of the Venusberg and the hope of forgiveness and redemption. Tannhäuser's dilemma had recently been the subject of a characteristically sardonic poem in Heine's extended essay *Elementargeister*, while the song contest had featured in stories by Tieck and Hoffmann. Wagner absorbed all of this into the compost heap of his imagination. As if this stimulation were not enough, at around the same time he came across a study of the legend of Lohengrin, the Swan Knight, son of Parzival and guardian of the Holy Grail. Here in Paris, a whole new world opened up to him – a whole new German world. The idea of Germany was growing apace. Beyond the classical achievements of the German Enlightenment – Goethe, Schiller, Lessing – there was a sense of a more or less mythical time when all German-speaking peoples were one, united by common assumptions, common experience. There was a distant memory of a pagan past, of a culture of nomadic warriors, whose lives were predicated based on a sort of heroic pessimism: there is no escape, in myths of these people, from recurring patterns of revenge and destruction. Connecting to all of this, Wagner felt his self-respect returning.

In his imagination, that is. The actual position was that at the age of twenty-eight, he had written four operas, only one of which had been performed, and that only once, and in chaotic circumstances. Three other operas, one of them four hours long, the second six, and the third of more modest duration, remained unperformed. He had no prospects and, cripplingly, no money. But then everything suddenly started to look up.

FOUR

Triumph

In quick succession, and thanks largely to Meyerbeer's persuasive championship, *Rienzi* was accepted for production by Dresden, and *The Flying Dutchman* by Berlin. In April 1842, after two and a half years of frustration, rejection and abject poverty in Paris, the Wagners set off for Dresden in triumph. The weather grew wintry as they headed eastward, away from the City of Light and towards driving snow and rain, but as they passed the Wartburg castle at Eisenach, home of the Minnesingers' contest, they found it flooded in sunshine. 'The view so warmed my heart against wind and weather, Jews and the Leipzig Fair,' he said, 'that I arrived safe and sound.' In which particular way Jews had exacerbated his temper Wagner does not specify – merely by existing, no doubt – but the symbolism of the sunshine in that particular place was profound for him: it was in Eisenach that Martin Luther translated the New Testament into German, and it was there that Johann Sebastian Bach had been born. This was the German heartland, and the sun was shining on it. Once in Dresden, Wagner rolled up his sleeves and got to work. The first thing he did was to start cutting large chunks of the score he nicknamed 'The Monster', then started rehearsing intensely with his two leading singers: Wilhelmine Schröder-Devrient, no less, as the page Adriano, and the trumpet-voiced tenor Joseph Tichatschek as Rienzi. The entire company was enchanted by the score; they so loved the rum-ti-tum finale to Act III that whenever there was a run through of it in rehearsal, everyone put a silver penny in a pot for the composer. None of them realised, he said, that had it not been for those silver pennies he would never have survived the rehearsal period.

The first performance was a roaring triumph. 'In trying to recall my condition that evening,' he wrote, 'I can remember it possessing all the features of a dream.' The audience, swept away by the splendid tunes, the heroic singing and the spectacular staging, applauded and cheered throughout a piece which, Wagner noted with rising anxiety, was, despite his savage cuts, very long indeed. The first two acts, which included a thirty-minute ballet, were as long as the whole of Weber's *Der Freischütz*. By the end of Act III it had clocked up four hours; the final curtain fell six hours after it had first risen. The following day, Wagner went to the theatre, possessed, despite the acclaim he had received, by a blind raging determination to strike out great chunks of what he called his 'convolution of monstrosities', bringing it down to a tolerable length. But the theatre and Tichatschek were appalled, refusing to allow him to cut a note. The success of the first night was repeated night after night; even the usually frosty Saxon royal family became fans. It was Wagner's first success, and nothing of his ever again received quite such unqualified approbation. But even as he was writing it he knew that he had outgrown its grandstanding style; he was already, in *The Flying Dutchman*, pushing towards a different kind of opera. The Dresden theatre, exhilarated by the unprecedented popularity of *Rienzi*, now asked Berlin for the privilege of giving the premiere of *Dutchman*, which was granted; the first performance duly took place a mere three months after the debut of *Rienzi*.

Nobody understood it. Despite the triumphant presence of Schröder-Devrient as Senta, for the rest, as far as acting was concerned, it was woefully undercast; whole tranches of the first act passed by with no dramatic engagement whatever from the performers. The hearty histrionics that made *Rienzi* go with such a swing were death to *The Flying Dutchman*, which needed detailed, psychologically credible acting and subtle vocal colours. Above all, it needed an imaginative involvement from the singers, which no one but Schröder-Devrient was capable of. In the pit, Wagner made sure that the overture was electrifying, plunging the audience into the howling storms he had so vividly conjured up, but until Senta's suicide leap at the end shook the audience from its lethargy, the dark and desperate story itself made little impact on the Dresden audience.

Nonetheless, the continuing afterglow of *Rienzi* was enough to confirm Wagner's status in Dresden, to the extent that, to Minna's inexpressible joy and relief, he was now offered the post of Royal Conductor, a position with a lifelong annual salary and involving only modest duties. He almost immediately regretted accepting the job, he said, because his sudden new visibility brought all his creditors out of the woodwork, people from the most distant parts of his life who thought they had, and who probably did have, a claim on him. Some dated back to his student days – some his school days – until at last he cried out that any day now he expected to receive a bill from the nurse that suckled him. He focussed on his new duties, conducting both his own works and those of others, notably a highly charged performance of Weber's *Euryanthe*, about which he had once been so rude. His absolute certainty about what he wanted and his ruthlessness in achieving it are remarkable – he was just thirty years old, had conducted a couple of seasons in some distinctly ropey provincial opera houses, and nothing at all during the last two and a half years. But the moment he arrived in Dresden he took the revered Royal Opera orchestra by the scruff of its neck and forced them to play the way he wanted. He insisted above all that they play with *meaning*; routine was intolerable to him. Expressiveness was everything. Naturally, they loathed him –

to begin with, at least. But other people sat up. They saw that Wagner was something quite out of the ordinary, and they gave him loyal support. These were his first disciples, inspired both to champion and to protect him; from now on, he would always be surrounded by acolytes, with whom his relationship was, like everything else in his life, complicated. The curious combination of masculine and feminine elements in his nature – of ruthlessness and vulnerability, of attack and seduction – created relationships with his supporters which were unnaturally intense and frequently ended badly.

In Dresden, in the early days, at any rate, he required neither protection nor championship: his job, being far from burdensome, afforded him plenty of time for reading. For the first time in his life he had exactly what he needed: time and money. He had been brooding over the story of Tannhäuser and finished writing the libretto – poem, as he insisted – exploring the minstrel's conflicting impulses, but within the context of a great debate about art, embodied in the Minnesingers' semi-historical song contest on the Wartburg. The artist was firmly at its centre – two artists, in fact, because Wagner had the remarkable idea of including among the characters the thirteenth-century poet and Minnesinger, Wolfram von Eschenbach, author of the great medieval German epic *Parzival*. He gave the opera the name *Venusberg*.

Shortly after finishing the libretto, he received one of those seismic shocks to his imagination to which he was so peculiarly prone. He came across Jacob Grimm's recently published study, *Teutonic Mythology*, and for the first time, agog, he encountered the Norse myths, the Eddas, the sagas of the Nibelungs and the Wälsungs. Greedily devouring the hefty tome, he experienced a sudden vertiginous plunge into the subconscious, finding things there which were at once completely new and long familiar:

The baldest legend spoke to me of its ancient home, and soon my whole imagination thrilled with images; long-lost forms for which I had sought so eagerly shaped themselves ever more and more clearly into realities that lived again. There rose up soon before my mind a whole world of figures, which revealed themselves as so strangely plastic and primitive that, when I saw them before me and heard their voices in my heart, I could not account for the almost tangible familiarity and assurance of their demeanour. The effect they produced upon the inner state of my soul I can only describe as an entire rebirth. Just as we feel a tender joy over a child's first bright smile of recognition, so now my own eye flashed with rapture as I saw a world, revealed, as it were, by miracle, in which I had hitherto moved blindly as the babe in its mother's womb.

He concluded that these unknown but familiar figures who spoke to him were his ancestors, the shadows, he said, of his own soul. Wagner was a Jungian before Jung; reading Grimm suddenly connected him to the collective unconscious. His inner life, for so long an unknown, disturbing territory to him, was becoming coherent. He was moving forward very rapidly. As far as he was concerned, *The Flying Dutchman* was the first real music he had ever written, the first music, as he put it, that he had written not from his conscious but from his unconscious mind. Its failure taught Wagner a lesson. The singers in the Dresden *Dutchman* had had no idea what to do with the music or the words he'd written for them. How could they? They'd never come across anything like it. He began to understand that, if the work he intended to write was to make its due effect, he was going to need a new kind of singer, a new kind of orchestral playing, a new kind of production, a new kind of theatre. Above all, he was going to need a new kind of audience, one educated by him. And he was going to have to do all this by himself – he understood that very clearly. It was a matter of willpower. 'To present a work in public,' he said, 'is to assert your superiority. The public resists. You have to fight and conquer them, win them over by violent efforts.'

These huge shifts in his inner life did not help him to write *Tannhäuser*, as he now called it; it was not coming easily. And they sat uncomfortably with his new respectability. Minna was thrilled to be the wife of the Royal Conductor, and busily set about furnishing their splendid new apartments appropriately: everything, Wagner noted scornfully, was good and substantial, as was only right, he noted with dread, for a man of thirty who was settling down at last for the rest of his life.

You can feel the rising panic, the claustrophobia as he describes his newfound stability. He has a magnificent grand piano, he has a fine writing desk, he has a library filled with works on German history, as well as the masterpieces of German literature, and those of ancient Greece, Italy, France and England. His plan was to work through them all, ideally in the original languages, none of which he spoke. But he was kept from his books by the small matter of having to compose *Tannhäuser* and attend new productions of *Rienzi* in Hamburg and *The Flying Dutchman* in Berlin, both of which, critically successful though they were, only confirmed him in his conviction of the hopelessness of the German operatic stage. *Rienzi* had meanwhile become a staple of the repertory in Dresden, and on the strength of it, some people had begun to speak of Wagner as the great white hope of German music. 'I am of the firm opinion that [*Rienzi*] is the finest thing achieved in grand opera in the last twelve years,' wrote the young critic Eduard Hanslick, who would before long come to articulate the opposition to Wagner, 'that it is the most significant dramatic creation since *Les Huguenots*, and that it is just as epoch-making for its own time as were *Les Huguenots*, *Der Freischütz* and *Don Giovanni*, each for its respective period of musical history.' These opinions were useful to Wagner, but he did not share them. He found the success of *Rienzi* pretty funny, in fact. To him it was passé, dead, history. He had moved on.

Encouraged by Minna, he took trouble to keep in with his royal employers, despite his essentially radical and revolutionary sympathies. His initial interview with Friedrich Augustus II was somewhat discouraging – the king amiably advised him to try to differentiate the characters in his operas rather better – but Wagner nonetheless developed a fondness for His Majesty. When the king came home from a sightseeing visit to England, the composer welcomed him back with a newly composed march: the celebrated march, in fact, from the as yet unfinished *Tannhäuser*, scored for 120 bandsmen with a 300-strong chorus from the local glee club. Wagner staged it himself – with unceasing activity and ever-present help, he says; no doubt he understates – arranging things so that at the second verse the performers processed off through the royal garden, gradually receding into the middle distance, allowing the final notes to reach the royal ears 'as an echoing dream-song'. It was a brilliant stroke of stage management, which enchanted the royal party, and enraged everyone else. Wagner had, in the most literal sense, stolen a march over those whose life's work it was to flatter their royal employers. From this point on, he became aware of undercurrents of resentment. His immediate boss, the director of the theatre, having earlier told him that he was a great man, and that he would soon be universally admired and loved, swiftly turned against him. 'Nevertheless,' Wagner remarked, 'a certain peculiar tenderness towards me on the part of this singular man was always clearly perceptible. Indeed, I might almost say that much of his subsequent abuse of me sounded more like the strangely perverted plaints of a love that met with no response.' It is entirely characteristic of Wagner to have seen the relationship in these terms; but it also seems, to a large extent, to have been true: all his life he provoked, almost flirtatiously, love and hate simultaneously. You never knew where you were with Wagner, which was how he liked it. Destabilisation was his primary modus operandi, in life as in art.

Even his feelings for the dead were complex. In Paris, he had turned against Weber, but now, newly converted to all things German, and filling the position Weber himself had once occupied, he enthusiastically committed himself to the ghoulish undertaking of returning his mortal remains to Dresden from London, where the great composer had died twenty years earlier after the disastrous first night of *Oberon* at Covent Garden. Wagner, determined to mark the great man's return with some splendour, specially composed two pieces for the exequies: the first a Berliozian *Funeral Symphony*, based on themes from *Euryanthe*, scored for eighty wind instruments, to accompany the ashes from the landing stage to the Catholic cemetery; the other a part-song for male voices to be performed at the grave the following day. The occasion was doubly sombre: the composer's son had died only a few days before. Weber's widow tearfully begged Wagner to postpone the event but he insisted that the ceremony must continue. He delivered the oration, too. This made a great effect. It was Wagner's first outing as a public speaker; more, much more, was to follow. Honouring Weber was not simple piety on his part: it publicly confirmed his embrace of all things German.

Meanwhile, he finished the score of *Tannhäuser*, and had it printed. Exhausted by his labours, he was ordered strict rest by the doctors and duly set off for Marienbad with Minna to take the waters; he was under strict instructions to avoid anything that might excite him. It was not to be. In his rucksack he had brought with him Eschenbach's medieval romances *Titurel* and *Parzival*, plus a story concerning Nuremberg's mastersingers which he'd found in a *History of German Literature*, along with another about the sixteenth-century cobbler-poet Hans Sachs. These utterly disparate stories, about Knights of the

Round Table in mythical Camelot, and craftsmen-singers in a bustling bourgeois community, swirled around and around in his imagination, until he felt compelled to find paper and pen and note down what were, in effect, the plot and characters of *Lohengrin* and *The Mastersingers of Nuremberg*. The doctors at the spa were highly displeased with all this activity and crossly told him that he was unfit for water cures.

Back in town, *Tannhäuser* was in rehearsal, and Wagner was forcefully reminded that he was now writing operas which demanded singers (and directors) who did not exist. Schröder-Devrient, cast as Venus, despite her ever-thickening girth and somewhat unstable vocal production, had what was needed: a powerful sense of character and passionate engagement with both text and music. But to explain the complex spiritual journey of Tannhäuser to the naïve giant Tichatschek, Wagner's original Rienzi, was a hopeless undertaking; to elucidate and dramatise the subtle shifts in the Song Contest in Act II impossible with the journeyman singers that were all the company could field. Wagner wanted to compel the audience – for the first time in the history of opera, he said – to take an interest in a poetical idea, by making them follow its every twist and turn. By miraculous good fortune, he found one singer in the resident company – just the one – who understood what he was talking about: the baritone Anton Mitterwurzer, who sang the pivotal role of Wolfram von Eschenbach. This shy, unsociable young man listened intently to what Wagner told him, at first with bafflement and frustration, finding himself unable to do what Wagner suggested, but going away every night and working towards it, until finally he had discovered a new way of singing and a new way of thinking; Wagner demanded nothing less. Mitterwurzer transformed himself in bearing, voice and appearance, convincing Wagner that it was, after all, possible to train singers to become artists; a natural genius like Schröder-Devrient might always come along, but he knew that his work would never make its proper impact until he had bred up a generation of new singers.

As far as *Tannhäuser* was concerned, two expressive, intelligent singers out of twenty was not enough. The first performance so deeply dismayed Wagner that he postponed the second for a week, during which time, in an effort to limit the damage Tichatschek's remorselessly jolly singing was inflicting on it, he made substantial cuts in the piece. By the third performance the theatre had a hit on its hands; Mitterwurzer, in particular, was acclaimed. But Wagner was profoundly dissatisfied. He had been trying to put onto the stage a story which had the power and poetry of the original sources. In Dresden, nothing – the scenery, the lighting, the singers' movements, their sense of character, their connection to the text – was remotely satisfactory. It was of no consolation to him that the singers sang well, or that the orchestra gave it their all: for *Tannhäuser* or *The Flying Dutchman* to work at all every element had to be right. Some years later, his frustration became so great that he insisted that whenever a company undertook to perform the score of *Tannhäuser*, a booklet of 'How To' instructions – *Tannhäuser* for Dummies – nicely bound in leather should be sent with it; *On the Performing of Tannhäuser*, was what he actually called it. It was not much appreciated. Not a single company to which the booklet had been sent, he noted, had even so much as opened it, which is a shame, because it is a remarkably clear guide to how the piece works, physically, musically and in terms of character. It shows, with great precision, how all these things are mutually interdependent and that the loss of any one of them means the collapse of them all. It reveals the degree to which, perhaps uniquely among opera composers, he saw that the theatrical manifestation of the work was not a bonus or an embellishment – it *was* the work. Everything in Wagner's operas is theatrically conceived; they are as far from pure music as can be imagined. Context is all. And he understood very clearly that theatre, musical or otherwise, is always a collaborative art; all the participants have to be involved, bringing their intelligence with them. He proposed – an unheard of suggestion, which would be radical even today – that before musical rehearsals had even begun, the singers (including the chorus) should sit down and read the whole libretto out loud, approaching the text as actors would approach a play, striving to make it as natural and as real and as characterful as possible. 'What I ask of the performer,' he says in the booklet, 'will certainly not be drummed into him by sheer weight of talk; and the whole course of study laid down by me, especially the holding of reading-rehearsals, aims at making the performer a fellow-feeling, a fellow-knowing, and finally, from his own convictions, a fellow-creative partner in the production.' He was asking a great deal of the theatre of his time, where such ideas were so far from conventional practice as to be thought almost risible. But he stuck at it, as he stuck at everything. And in the end, he transformed the entire approach to what he was already describing not as opera, but as music-drama.

In Dresden he associated with the intellectual *crème de la crème*; but he soon tired of their elegant polemics. They were, he felt, nonentities, and as often as not, he pleasantly remarked, Jewish nonentities. After *Tannhäuser* he was in the grip of intense, if frustrated, creative energy; he felt impelled to compose something to rid himself of the disturbing and painful excitement writing it had produced in him. Composition for Wagner caused a neurotic disturbance within which could only be cured by more composition. Out of the several projects simmering on the hob of his creative imagination, it was the story of Lohengrin which spoke to him most urgently. He started to write the poem – the libretto – immediately after the premiere of *Tannhäuser*; it was done in four weeks. In it, the hero, clad in bright shining armour, appears in a boat drawn by a swan, as if in answer to Elsa of Brabant's dream of a champion who will save her from the cruel attentions of a man she hates. The swan-knight promises to marry her, as long as she never asks his name or where he has come from; he then fells the man who has been tormenting her, but spares his life. The knight from nowhere and Elsa marry; but she is unable to resist asking his name, whereupon he abandons her: they can never be together as man and wife. In parting he reveals his identity: he is Lohengrin, a Knight of the Grail, and the son of Parzival. Sorrowfully, he bids Elsa farewell, and prepares to leave on the boat that brought him, drawn, as before, by a swan. As he is about to leave, the Holy Grail hovers over the swan, which sinks into the water, to be replaced by Elsa's lost brother, into whose arms she sinks, lifeless. If *Tannhäuser* was about the makers of myth, *Lohengrin* is myth itself.

Wagner read the libretto out loud, as he always did, to his friends and colleagues. The effect on them was overwhelming. More than one member of his little audience said that had he chosen to be an actor, he would have been the greatest of them all: people wept, they were compelled, disturbed, elated. And all this without a note of music. Schumann was among Wagner's audience on that occasion; he was duly impressed. He had no doubt that Wagner was a remarkable composer, but found his volubility exhausting: 'He possesses a tremendous gift of the gab and is full of oppressive ideas,' he noted in his diary. 'It's impossible to listen to him for any length of time.' Wagner, for his part, admired Schumann but found him baffling: 'you can't converse with Schumann … he never says anything'. Despite the success of the reading, Wagner was not yet ready to compose the music to *Lohengrin*; instead he immersed himself in yet more study – history, mythology, literature. He was especially taken by the Grimm Brothers' great compilation of the factual records of German life in the

Middle Ages. And, as so often when he wanted to drink deep from the well of German art, he turned to Beethoven, announcing his intention of conducting the opera orchestra, chorus and soloists in the Ninth Symphony.

The proposal met with immediate resistance. The work was virtually unknown in Dresden – the orchestra was nervous of it – no one would come to hear it – the only other time they had done it, it had been an embarrassing disaster – Beethoven's last scores were known to be the work of a madman, a deaf madman, at that. Undaunted, Wagner proceeded with his plan. But first, before approaching the performers, he had to work on himself. In some mysterious way, he said, he identified with the score, as if it were a fragment of his own spiritual autobiography. This made for an emotional period of study. Anyone who had come upon him unexpectedly, he said, convulsed with sobs and tears, with the score open on his desk before him, might reasonably have asked if this was really fitting behaviour in the Conductor Royal of Saxony. Studying the score helped him to accept something he had previously been unable to admit to himself: how profoundly insecure he was both artistically and emotionally. Working on the symphony would somehow, he felt, exorcise this insecurity, dispel this anxiety.

When he was good and ready, and not a day before, he announced a lengthy schedule of rehearsals with the orchestra. He was determined to ensure that every strand of the work was given its due expressive weight. When, occasionally, Beethoven had, in Wagner's view, got it wrong, he helped him out, clarifying or augmenting the orchestration as necessary. He worked with infinite patience to perfect the work's many problematic sections. For the famously treacherous recitative passage for lower strings at the beginning of the last movement, he allowed an astounding twelve rehearsals, so that the orchestra could play it not only with complete freedom but also with exquisite tenderness and inner energy. Mitterwurzer made his electrifying intervention in the last movement, the baritone soloist's great call to arms – 'Friends! Not these sounds!' – with all the flexibility of expression and focus on meaning he had learned as Wolfram in *Tannhäuser*. For this finale, Wagner beefed up the chorus to 300, reinforcing the Academy of Singing with choirs from the Kreuzschule and the Dresden Seminary, working them up into what he called 'the correct state of ecstasy'. He demonstrated to the basses over and over again, until his own weak and rasping voice was spent, the feeling of rapture called for in 'Be embraced, ye countless millions', the tiny Napoleonic figure urging his forces on to greater and greater heights with a potent combination of high feeling and meticulous precision.

Preparing the performers was not enough: Wagner knew he had to prepare his audience, too, to teach them how to approach the work. Deploying the highly advanced showman's instincts that were the obverse of his fanatical commitment to high art, he placed anonymous teasers – stories from rehearsals and so on – in the influential Dresden daily paper, the *Anzeiger*, in an attempt to pique the audience's curiosity. He personally wrote the programme booklet, filling it with suggestions as to what he believed was the hidden programme of the music, echoing E. T. A. Hoffmann's technicolored analyses of Beethoven:

> At the heart of the first movement seems to lie a struggle of titanic proportions, in which the soul, striving for joy, wrestles against the oppression of that hostile power that interposes itself between us and earthly happiness. The mighty principal theme, which steps forward at the very beginning, naked and powerful, as if from behind some unearthly veil, could perhaps without detriment to the spirit of the work as a whole be translated by Goethe's words: *Renunciation! –* Learn, man, to *forgo!*

Goethe's *Faust* was the key to Wagner's understanding of the music. Throughout the programme booklet he laced his commentary with quotations from the great play-poem, framing the symphony in the epic context of Man's struggle with himself. Faust, probing, questioning, lurching manic-depressively from ecstasy as he contemplates the wonder of creation to abject despair at the impossibility of engaging directly with its primal energy, is the German Hamlet; Wagner, with his own deep instability, saw himself clearly in the figure of the philosopher. In his Parisian journalism, he had already scornfully rejected rule-bound erudition: formal learning – 'our German curse'; Faust, too, bitterly dismisses the way of scholarship, which he feels has lied to him and cheated him, giving him mere knowledge without power. Instead, he embraces direct exposure to the dazzling truths that underpin life itself. In Paris, Wagner had started work on a *Faust* symphony of which only the first movement, a portrait of Faust himself oscillating between ecstasy and despair, survived in the form of an intensely evocative overture; to it he attached a Goethean epigraph:

> ... The indwelling spirit
> Whose temple is my heart, who rules its powers,
> Can stir the bosom to its lowest depths,
> But has no power to move external nature,
> And therefore is existence burdensome,
> And death desirable, and life detested.

This is the heroically unsettled spirit he discerned in Beethoven's last symphony. In the programme booklet, he sought to illuminate the sublime slow movement with a further quotation from Faust's huge monologue at the beginning of the play, a despairing survey of his life which leads him to the brink of suicide, from which he is only pulled back by the sound of the Easter bells:

I do not ask for joy.
I take the way of turmoil's bitterest gain,
I sicken, long revolted at all learning;
Then let us quench the pain of passion's burning
In the soft depth of sensual delight.
Now let your muffled mysteries emerge,
Breed magic wonders naked to our glance,
Now plunge we headlong in time's racing surge,
Swung on the sliding wave of circumstance.
Bring now the fruits of pain or pleasure forth,
Sweet triumph's lure, or disappointment's wrath,
A man's dynamic needs this restless urge.

Such were the thoughts with which he prepared his listeners for the experience they were about to undergo. This was no mere concert – it was intended to be a life-changing experience. Now, with the intellectual, spiritual and musical preparations complete, it was necessary to ensure that every note of the music so carefully and passionately prepared reached the ears of the audience with maximum impact, so he turned himself into an acoustician, reconstructing the whole concert platform, converting the rectilinear hall into a semi-circular amphitheatre, with the choir raised behind the orchestra, surrounding it.

His work paid off spectacularly. The audience was staggered, knocked sideways by a piece they had expected to find risible. In effect, with this and his many subsequent performances of Beethoven's Ninth, he not only transformed the reputation of the piece, turning it, for more than a hundred years, into what was universally believed to be the pinnacle of Western classical music, he also invented the modern art of conducting, working with the musicians as a director works with actors, not simply co-ordinating them but compelling them to engage with the meaning behind the notes. Creating the notion of the conductor as puppet master, he aggregated all power into his own hands, controlling every element, infusing it with his own vision, co-creating with the composer. 'You seemed to me like a god,' Minna wrote to him after the concert, 'ruling the mighty elements and bewitching the audience.' There were fine conductors before Wagner – his fellow composers Spohr, Mendelssohn, Schumann and Liszt had brought formidable intelligence and profound musicality to the task. But Wagner was the first of the maestros, the conductor-wizards, the alchemists of the orchestra.

What he had done, in effect, was to dramatise the music, to make it tell a story: his story. He knew the scale of what he had achieved. By sheer force of will, he had galvanised recalcitrant and sceptical performers and a resistant audience. This experience with Beethoven's Ninth confirmed in him the belief that if he wanted anything enough, he could get it. How to transfer this success to his proper sphere, that of the opera house? And in particular, the production of his own works? He got close to what he was after in a production of Gluck's *Iphigenia in Aulis*, for which he composed new recitatives, re-orchestrating the piece, reshaping it to make it coherent, both musically and emotionally. In preparation for this, he had read deeply in ancient Greek history and culture, becoming ever more obsessed by it. He felt that he could not understand German culture until he had begun again, as he said, from the beginning. He read Plato. He read every extant Greek play, delighting above all in Aeschylus and, perhaps less predictably, Aristophanes. He immersed himself in world history, reading Gibbon's *Decline and Fall of the Roman Empire*, Niebuhr's *Roman History* and *The History of Greek Heroes* and Plutarch's *Life of Alexander*. And then, to re-Germanise himself, he moved on to the Scandinavian sagas and the commentaries.

And at the same time, he was composing *Lohengrin*. It is, like *Tannhäuser*, like *The Flying Dutchman*, a story of redemption, but this time illuminated by the irradiating power of the Holy Grail. To express this power he summoned up from the profoundest depths of his imagination a palette of sound like nothing that had ever been conjured from any orchestra ever before. Wagner described the overture in unabashedly narrative and pictorial terms:

> Out of the clear blue ether of the sky there seems to condense a wonderful, yet at first hardly perceptible, vision; and out of this there gradually emerges, ever more and more clearly, an angel-host bearing in its midst the sacred Grail. As it approaches earth, it pours out exquisite odours, like streams of gold, ravishing the senses of the beholder. The glory of the vision grows and grows until it seems as if the rapture must be shattered and dispersed by the very vehemence of its own expansion. The vision draws nearer, and the climax is reached when at last the Grail is revealed in all its glorious reality, radiating fiery beams and shaking the soul with emotion. The beholder sinks on his knees in adoring self-annihilation. The Grail pours out its light on him like a benediction, and consecrates him to its service; then the flames gradually die away, and the angel-host soars up again to the ethereal heights in tender joy, having made pure once more the hearts of men by the sacred blessing of the Grail.

This is how he conceived of his own music. It was twelve years before he was to hear it.

FIVE

The World in Flames

At the beginning of 1848, as Wagner put the finishing touches to his new opera, the world was falling apart again, insurrection erupting volcanically all across Europe like Holy Fire. Wagner's old revolutionary sympathies flickered back to life. He had rejoiced when attempts to restore the old dispensation had been thwarted in Austria, where students and workers had fought side by side. Wagner celebrated his newfound solidarity by quickly knocking off an incendiary poem which a prominent Viennese newssheet printed. In Saxony, meanwhile, Friedrich Augustus II responded to events by installing a new liberal ministry, which put a fully democratic constitution in place. Not everybody was convinced. Popular opinion in Dresden quickly polarised between constitutional monarchists and out-and-out republicans. The latter established a party which called itself the Patriotic Union (Vaterlands-Verein); August Röckel, Wagner's associate conductor at the Court Theatre, was its leading spirit. Röckel invited Wagner to air his views, which – his taste for public speaking having been whetted by the Weber celebrations – he was only too willing to do.

Addressing some 3,000 people, Wagner argued for a form of constitutional monarchy in which the king was an equal with his subjects; as part of the new dispensation, what he called 'the demonic concept of money' would be abolished. The speech roused his listeners to wild enthusiasm, especially passages concerning the 'sycophantic' courtiers by whom the king, he said, was surrounded: this was particularly gratifying, of course, coming from the Orchestral Conductor Royal and it went round the city like wildfire. The excitement of the event seems to have gone to Wagner's head. Never popular in court circles, he was now acquiring serious enemies; that night at the theatre he was due to conduct *Rienzi*, of all things, with its spectacular scenes of popular turbulence. He was warned that there might well be a demonstration against him; instead, he was greeted with a roar of approval. The press entered the fray on the other side, along with the court officials who had borne the brunt of his coruscating oratory; for them he was public enemy number one. He quickly knocked off a letter to the king, pleading thoughtless indiscretion rather than deliberate offence, and was assured that, despite pressure from courtiers, his job was safe. He went to Vienna to try, unsuccessfully, to whip up a production of something of his own there; failing to do so, he seized the opportunity of dropping in on a meeting of one of the most radical groups in the city, blissfully oblivious that his every move was being monitored and reported.

Wagner returned to Dresden to discover the entirely unsurprising fact that there were intrigues afoot to eject him from the Court Theatre. Instead of lying low, he sought out Röckel, now dismissed from his job at the theatre and editing a firebrand socialist newspaper; Wagner felt an urgent need to discuss the political situation with him. Persuaded by Röckel's arguments, he became increasingly radicalised, connecting his idealistic views of the position of art in society with Röckel's vision of a world where the power of capital was annihilated, and class, position and family prejudices would disappear. In the new order, Röckel assured him, everybody would participate in labour according to their strength and capacity, work would cease to be a burden and would eventually assume a purely artistic character.

Inspired by all this, Wagner drew up a plan for a national theatre which would be independent of the court, and approached some of the radical new deputies to discuss it.

They gave him to understand that determining the position of art, or theatre, in the new world they were seeking to bring into being was a rather low priority. Shortly after, he participated in a musical gala at which he conducted the tumultuous, ecstatic finale to Act I of *Lohengrin* – the first time it had been heard in public. Trumpets blaze and cymbals crash as the king and his men hail the swan-borne hero:

> Raise a song of victory
> loud in highest praise to the hero!
> Acclaimed be your journey!
> Praised be your coming!
> Hail to your name,
> protector of virtue!
> You have defended
> the right of the innocent;
> praised be your coming!
> Hail to your race!
> To you alone we sing in celebration,
> to you our songs resound!
> Never will a hero like you
> come to this land again!

The women join in, singing:

> O that I could find songs of rejoicing
> to match his fame,
> worthy to acclaim him,
> rich in highest praise!
> You have defended
> the right of the innocent;
> praised be your
> coming!
> Hail to your journey!

This viscerally exciting, headlong climax to the first act of Wagner's as yet unperformed piece was greeted with muted applause. Nonetheless, he made a fiery speech, sharing with his fellow guests his vision of how the members of the orchestra might be directly and democratically involved in their own destinies. The applause for this was even more muted than for *Lohengrin*. Heinrich Marschner, composer of *The Vampire*, who was sitting at the same table, drily expressed doubts as to the desire or ability of orchestral musicians to function democratically. The revolution in the arts, he felt, would not be so easily achieved. In the streets outside the concert hall, revolution seemed all too probable. They were milling with demonstrators, among them Austrian dissidents Wagner had met during his recent visit to the radical cell in Vienna. They appeared at the theatre one night asking for tickets for *Rienzi*, which he duly arranged. That night in the theatre, and indeed whenever *Rienzi* and *Tannhäuser* were performed, Wagner was cheered to the echo. He had become something of a popular hero. He knew this could bode no good for him, so he was deeply surprised when, during this period of political uncertainty, he was asked by the Opera Intendant to submit *Lohengrin* for production. The offer was withdrawn almost immediately: the court was now, as he suspected, implacably opposed to him.

Against this incandescent backdrop, he continued to discharge his duties as conductor punctiliously, conducting Bellinis and Meyerbeers as required; but the theatre, with all its inadequacies and intrigues, utterly disgusted him: he was now dead to the job. As the political situation grew edgier by the day, he started writing a new libretto based on a story of which, he said, he had been half-afraid, but which now demanded to be written: the fifteenth-century saga of the Nibelungen, which describes the turbulent life and death of the great hero, Siegfried, against a backdrop of gods and dwarves, dragons and giants. Writing flat out, he compressed the vast mass of material into a fast-moving text, starting with Norns spinning the web of destiny, and ending with Rhinemaidens reclaiming the gold stolen from them by the Nibelungs, as Brünnhilde, lover of Siegfried and daughter of Wotan, chief of the gods, triumphantly conveys her lover's dead body to heaven in her chariot. Despite its provenance, Wagner's libretto was no antique fable: in it he was graphically describing what he saw all around him: the collapse of the old world order. *Siegfried's Death*, he called it; he wrote as if possessed. And then, as an afterthought, he knocked off a treatment for a play about Jesus Christ as a social revolutionary.

He knew that his tenure at Dresden could not last much longer. On Palm Sunday 1849, despite the ever-growing turmoil all around, he went ahead with the scheduled performance of Beethoven's Ninth Symphony; the finale, with its great hymn to brotherly love – *'Seid umschlungen, millionen!'* ('Be embraced, you millions!') had an overwhelming – a desperate – intensity; spurred on by him, singers and players rose heroically to what he had said was required: 'the correct state of ecstasy'.

> Joy, O wondrous spark divine,
> Daughter of Elysium,
> Drunk with fire now we enter,
> Heavenly one, your holy shrine.
> Your magic powers join again
> What fashion strictly did divide;
> Brotherhood unites all men
> Where your gentle wings spread wide.

During the fervent applause that followed, a colossal, bearded figure suddenly emerged from the audience. It was the Russian anarchist, Mikhail Bakunin, the most notorious terrorist in the world, the Osama bin Laden of his day, with a hefty bounty on his head. He strode down to the orchestra pit and, turning to the audience, announced in a loud voice that 'even if everything else is going to be destroyed in the coming conflagration, we must save this'. Wagner had first met Bakunin at Röckel's, where he had listened, half-enthralled, half-appalled, as the great bearded giant calmly proclaimed the destruction of the world: London, Paris, St Petersburg, all reduced to rubble. What place would art have then? Wagner thought to himself. He found it unbearable to contemplate the demolition of his ideals and hopes for the future of art, and yet the destruction of a corrupt and discredited world order was irresistibly attractive. Bakunin provoked constantly fluctuating emotions in Wagner: from involuntary horror to magnetic attraction, a not entirely dissimilar reaction to the emotions he himself provoked in others.

The political situation was heading towards a catastrophe. Wagner confessed to experiencing a strong impulse just to give himself over to the stream of events, wherever it might lead, as he had done twenty years earlier during the 1830 riots; something fundamentally inchoate in his temperament was excited by movement of any kind, activity, explosions, destruction. Things were moving at a giddying pace. Parliament had been dissolved by a new, reactionary ministry; Röckel was forced to escape. Wagner took over the running of his newspaper, the *Volksblätter* (the People's Press); at a committee meeting of the Vaterlands-Verein which Wagner attended as the paper's representative, there was a practical discussion about weapons, who should bear them and when. Wagner was loudly in favour of issuing guns to all the revolutionaries. In the middle of the discussion the tocsin bell sounded and they all rushed out onto the street. Wagner headed straight to Tichatschek's house to borrow his rifle, but the singer, a keen hunter, was on holiday and had taken it with him. Frau Tichatschek was in a state of terror at what might happen – perfectly reasonable in the circumstances, but her fear unaccountably provoked Wagner to uncontrollable laughter. Over the next few days he allowed himself, unarmed, to be carried along by the crowd, keenly interested, but not participating, he said, though there is evidence that he and Röckel had ordered a substantial number of powerful hand grenades from the iron-founder Oehme; supposedly intended for Prague, they were in fact kept in the *Volksblätter* offices, where Oehme primed them.

As the situation grew more and more dangerous, the government appealed to Prussia for help in controlling it. There was a move among the radicals to persuade the Saxon troops to declare for the parliament. Wagner impulsively organised a demonstration in favour of this, getting the paper's printer to run up a banner for him emblazoned with the words 'ARE YOU ON OUR SIDE AGAINST THE FOREIGN TROOPS?' As he stood holding the banner, out of the corner of his eye he saw Bakunin strolling around, chewing a cigar, and scoffing at the feebleness of the improvised barricades. A couple of days later, a large crowd proclaimed a pan-German constitution. Despite these dramatic developments, people continued ambling unhurriedly about the streets. It all felt like a fascinating piece of theatre, Wagner said, until the terrifyingly proficient Prussian troops arrived and shooting started in earnest. When this happened, Wagner climbed up the Kreuzkirche Tower in the centre of town to get a clear view of what was going on – or to save his bacon; either or both is possible. He kept vigil there all through the night, while the tower's great bell clanged incessantly, and the Prussian rifle shot beat against its walls. The following day, after some particularly violent skirmishes, the old Opera House, the scene for Wagner of so much misery, intrigue, and frustration, went up in flames, which gave him deep satisfaction; the fire seemed to have taste, he noted, because once it had consumed the unlovely Opera House, it stopped short of the beautiful Natural History Museum and the formidable armoury. On Sunday morning he went home, to Minna, and their house in the suburbs, but later that day he went back to Dresden, irresistibly drawn to the battle, which the insurrectionaries were now losing. A provisional government had been established under the leadership of Otto Leonard Heubner; he had appointed Bakunin as his adviser. But this was fantasy: backed by the Prussian military, the Saxon government swiftly regained control and the revolution was over before it had begun.

Bakunin, Röckel and their colleague Heubner fled by carriage to the Saxon city of Chemnitz for safety, but they were betrayed, arrested and condemned to death. Wagner was following just behind them in a second carriage; seeing what had happened to Bakunin, he hopped carriages and made a swift exit to the adjacent state of Weimar, where Franz Liszt – staunch champion of the musical avant-garde, whom Wagner had befriended in Paris – was planning, as 'Kapellmeister Extraordinaire' to the court, to stage *Tannhäuser*.

On arrival in Weimar, Wagner was warmly embraced by Liszt, and even shook hands with the art-loving grand duke and duchess, who were courtesy itself. It soon became apparent, however, that he would not be able to stay there: all the states of the German Confederation – including, in its polite, apologetic way, Weimar – were fiercely united against revolutionaries, and that was what Wagner was now. He had a secret meeting at the border with a tearful Minna, who was understandably reproachful: their comfortable, respectable life in Dresden, everything she had ever dreamed of for them, gone, and for what? But Wagner had no time to dawdle; flight was imperative. Liszt supplied him with a false passport, and he was smuggled out of the country in the guise of a certain 'Professor Widmann'. This subterfuge appealed to Wagner immensely. Widmann, his passport declared, was Swabian, and so, with typically madcap humour Wagner, at this moment of possibly mortal peril, did his best to affect a Swabian accent. It defeated him; happily, none of the border guards noticed, and he slipped onto the waiting steamer. Before long he was on neutral Swiss soil, in Zurich. It was eleven years before he next set foot in Germany; and another two years after that before he was admitted back to Saxony.

SIX

Pause for Thought

If, as he says, he sleepwalked into the revolution, he now had a sharp awakening. He was an exile, a fugitive, and a marked man; the Saxon government issued a warrant for his arrest which applied across the confederation. Soon after arriving in Switzerland he went to Paris, but with only rudimentary French and all his contacts exhausted, he was wasting his time there. So back to Zurich he went. For a while he was exhilarated at what he called his bird-like freedom, though he admitted that even he was sometimes frightened by the outbursts of manic exuberance which accompanied his crazed, paradox-filled conversational riffs. On and on he talked, about art and revolution, about the theatre of the future, about the German soul, about politics, about history. Eventually, when people stopped listening, he started to write it all down, groping towards some sort of personal philosophy. He found a publisher in Leipzig who brought out his first extended pamphlet under the sensational title of *Art and Revolution*; largely because it was by a former Royal Kapellmeister and now notorious political refugee, it quickly went into a second edition.

In it and its many, many successors he was essentially talking to himself, thinking out loud. He was thirty-seven, and he'd written six lengthy operas, three of which are now cornerstones of the operatic repertory. But as far as he was concerned, he'd hardly begun. He knew that *Tannhäuser* and *Lohengrin*, for all their originality of orchestration, for all the heightened emotion, for all their high seriousness, were the end of a road for him; they were constructed according to what he now thought of as a discredited plan – arias, duets, ensembles, choruses, following one another with no unitary dramatic cohesion. But what should take its place? What kind of opera did he want to write? If he was to write the work of art of the future, as he fervently intended, he needed to be very clear about what it was. Exiled, of utterly uncertain future, he decided to write no more music until he had achieved that clarity. It took him five years.

For a man out of whom music had poured unstoppably for fifteen years, simply to switch off the flow and take stock for five entire years borders on the heroic. But there was no alternative. He was incapable of writing another note until he knew where he was coming from. So now he had some very hard thinking to do, and, being Wagner, he had to do it out loud, in a flood of pamphlets, essays, books. They are diffuse, repetitive, often obscure, but they faithfully convey what Wagner believed he was doing, had done and was about to do. Taken together, they add up to a major body of theoretical work unlike that of any other major composer, encompassing far more than music. This was the way his mind worked. He needed to articulate these things in order to move forward. What were the principles that informed the highest art? He probed this question relentlessly over five years of tireless reading, thinking, expounding. It is hard to think of any other great creative artist who has challenged him- or herself in this way. In order to achieve the clarity he needed, he fiercely drove his largely self-educated brain. He was an omnivorous reader, especially in philosophy and philology, though he was completely untrained in either. He believed that there was a Holy of Holies, an ultimate truth, to which all of his thinking and all of his creative energies were directed. But what was it? He was painfully aware that he had wasted his student years and was forever trying to make up

lost ground, which made him almost promiscuously susceptible to new ideas.

Approaching the great thinkers of the modern age, he
started with Hegel. He was awestruck by what he called the
mysterious power of the philosopher's writing, a power he
thought comparable to Beethoven's in his Ninth Symphony,
but, on his own admission, he barely understood a word of it.
Then his attention was drawn by a Catholic priest and political agitator named Menzdorff to the work of Ludwig
Feuerbach; Feuerbach, Menzdorff told him, was 'the only real
philosopher of modern times'. Wagner eagerly seized on the
philosopher's first book, *Thoughts on Death and Immortality*,
finding it a model of lucidity after Hegel. This he could understand, and it gave him a massive jolt. He fervently embraced
its proposition that individual human consciousness is part of
an infinite consciousness into which it will be absorbed at
death, and that belief in immortality and a personal deity are
merely expressions of egoism. What he saw as the tragic
dimension of this argument appealed greatly to Wagner.
Above all, he endorsed Feuerbach's rejection of the tyranny of
accepted ideas based on a blind belief in authority. Authority
had been the bane of Wagner's life, humiliating him and
acting as a check on the free expanse of his creative spirit – 'art
made tongue-tied by authority', as Shakespeare has it. Oscar
Wilde's observation that, 'the form of government that is most
suitable to the artist is no government at all', exactly expresses
Wagner's sentiments. Authority was the problem; it should
simply be abolished, because, left to their own devices, people
naturally live together in productive harmony. Power was
mankind's great enemy. Thus he worked himself round to
Bakunin's anarchist position. He warmed particularly to
Feuerbach's contention that the best philosophy was to have
no philosophy, and that only what could be ascertained by
the senses was real, thus abolishing the authority even of

philosophy. This translated into a mandate for the demolition of society's structures.

Art and Revolution is profoundly indebted to *Death and Immortality*, most notably in its enthusiasm for communism – a coinage of Feuerbach's. But then his enthusiasm began to wane. The philosopher's next book, *The Essence of Christianity*, rocked the religious establishment to its foundations; Wagner dismissed it as prolix, and when presented with the book after that, *Lectures on the Essence of Religion*, he snapped it shut and cast it aside – terrified, he said, by the dullness of its title alone. Intellectually insatiable though he was, there was nothing dilettante about Wagner's approach to books. His aim was to create an all-embracing work of art, a perfect drama which would appeal to the simplest, deepest and most human emotions: that was what he meant by the 'Art-work of the Future', the title of another of his pamphlets. If he could use the ideas contained in the books he read to create that work, he would; if not, not.

Alternating in his mind with these lofty preoccupations was the ever-pressing question of money and how to get it. He was now no longer gainfully employed. Pretty well every second paragraph in Wagner's autobiography is about money. Although large sums of it, often paid on a regular basis, passed through his hands, it was never enough. Such performances of his works as took place rarely raised much by way of royalties; his journalism was modestly remunerated, and paid late; and since his rapid exit from Dresden he had no prospect of work as a conductor. He constantly made the rounds of his friends, begging bowl in hand; his own family, he said, treated him much as one treats an invalid by whom one dreads to become infected. Somehow money kept appearing. People were moved to proffer him loans, even regular allowances. These all came to an end, sooner or later, sometimes acrimoniously, sometimes with apologies, or else the money just disappeared into the great fathomless sump of his debt. After a few arid months in Zurich, he was so desperate that he went back to Paris, scene of his greatest humiliations, in the belief that someone was going to perform the overture to *Tannhäuser* (nobody did) and with a vague and unconvincing plan to write an opera for the city that had so comprehensively ignored him. Nothing came of that either. He was adopted by various young couples: the husbands would give him money and houses to live in; they were his patrons. The wives would receive his erotic attentions; they were his muses. This seemed to him to be an admirable and equitable arrangement. Alas, few husbands seemed to grasp the favour he was doing them and when the wealthy wine-merchant husband of one muse began to suspect (not altogether wrongly) that Wagner was amorously involved with his wife, and threatened to put a bullet through his head, he decided it was time to go back to Zurich.

Minna was waiting for him there. She had tried to find him in Paris, but he evaded her; later he wrote her a letter saying that he would perfectly understand if she wanted a divorce. It turned out that she didn't; she wanted to look after him, and at this moment in his life, he was prepared to be looked after. The unrelenting soap opera of his emotional life was too much even for him. He was not feeling too good about himself in general. In Paris, when he had heard the news of the death sentences passed on Bakunin, Heubner and Röckel after the Dresden uprising, he felt acutely that he should have been there in the dock with them, and determined to break with everything and everyone; he suddenly lost all desire to learn anything more about life or art. With a certain moody theatricality, he prepared *Siegfried's Death* for publication, adding a preface dedicating it to his friends 'as a relic of the time when I had hoped to devote myself entirely to art, and especially to the composition of music'. Henceforward, he said, he just wanted to trust to chance and put himself beyond the reach of everybody – in Greece, perhaps, or Asia Minor, where he hoped to forget and be forgotten. He had already spent time wandering aimlessly in the mountains, reading the *Odyssey*, with whose hero he naturally strongly identified.

Minna did a pretty good impersonation of Penelope, welcoming back her errant husband. She lavished all her considerable domestic skills on prettifying their modest accommodation. She had brought their little dog, Peps, and their parrot, with her. The parrot, which knew quite large chunks of *Rienzi* by heart, greeted Wagner when he came home by calling out his name, then whistled the finale of Beethoven's Fifth Symphony. The dog, by contrast, collapsed into paroxysms of howling and sobbing whenever addressed. An additional complication in the ménage was the presence of Nathalie, Minna's daughter, who, still believing that she was Minna's sister, resented the discipline which the older woman tried to exercise over her; she was twenty-five by now, and vicious spats between them were a regular part of daily life. Wagner learned to ignore what was going on around him, immersing himself ever more deeply in his reading.

Meanwhile *Lohengrin*, of which he had only ever heard the first act's finale, was about to be performed under Liszt's baton in Weimar, where of course Wagner was forbidden to go for fear of being arrested. Determined nonetheless to mark the occasion, on the opera's first night he and Minna went to stay in a hotel in Lucerne and sat, side by side, watching the hands of the clock go round, imagining each phase of the performance. Otherwise he diverted himself with conducting the modest forces of the Zurich Orchestra – 'my facility in interpreting music at that time', he casually remarks, 'attained a degree of perfection I had not hitherto reached' – and writing *Opera and Drama*, in which he makes his most complete statement concerning his vision. He read it out loud to his friends in Zurich over twelve consecutive evenings. Stuffed with the fruits of his reading over the previous decade, it is of almost impenetrable denseness; one can only admire the stamina of those early listeners. He had to write this book to push himself into the mental state necessary to create the vast work he was now planning: a piece of music-theatre on an unprecedented scale – epic beyond anything ever attempted in a theatre – which was both to pioneer and to exemplify the Art-work of the Future. Its basis would be *Siegfried's Death*; it would present a devastatingly dystopian vision of human society, built on the ur-myths of the German people: the stories of his tribe. His purpose was revolution, nothing less. Art would once more be the unifying, cohesive dynamo of society, refreshing and purifying its audiences – the People, that is, the Volk. In this it would be the direct heir to the Greek theatre. The work's profound grounding in German culture would guarantee its vitality and its authenticity. It would return to the roots of civilisation, embodied in the myths; spurning the merely realistic portrayal of human life, it would dig into the archetypes behind the surface, stirring up and confronting the deepest and darkest elements in man's psyche. It would supplant religion; it would renew democracy. All of this was laid out in *Opera and Drama*.

What he said was deeply radical. In the world of opera of 1850, the world of Gounod and Meyerbeer, it was seriously challenging, rigorous, hard-core stuff, as fundamental a rethink as Cubism. Or Darwin. Or Einstein. It'd be pretty radical today. To begin with, it appeared that he was not interested in writing opera at all. He saw himself, as he had done since *Leubald and Adelaïde*, not as a composer at all, but as a dramatist. All that interested him, he said, was the drama, of which opera as currently practised was a dilution and a perversion, swamped by superficial, purely musical effects. The decorative and the conventional were to be stripped away: texts would be set one note to a syllable; music should fulfil the text, not embellish it; its function was to express character, situation and intention in a series of recognisable musical motifs: character and action alone would drive the work. The job of the orchestra, meanwhile, was not simply to accompany or add colour to the sung texts: it would weave the musical motifs together in an almost infinite number of combinations, commenting on the action, underlining its meaning. Meaning was central to the drama. Wagner despised the idea of theatre as entertainment; but equally he despised the notion of art for art's sake. The Greeks had got it right, he said. Their drama was a communal act, a sacred event, in which the ancient stories of the tribe were played out, enabling the audience to confront the deepest, most sublime and most terrible truths of human life, producing a profound, an overwhelming, release – a catharsis – which was the whole point of the drama. The Greeks had achieved this with an irresistible fusion of the combined arts of acting, gesture, scenic effect, poetry and music – what he called *ein Gesamtkunstwerk*: a total work of art. Anything less was trivial and not worth his or anyone else's attention.

He knew perfectly well that none of the works he had so far written were in the league of Aeschylus or Sophocles. He would not stop until he had written something that was. This insistence on a return to ancient models was not motivated by reverence, much less by nostalgia. Wagner was no antiquarian. He was not in the least bit interested in resurrecting ancient forms of theatre. He believed that in his lifetime the drama had been emasculated, diminished, robbed of its potency, and that only a return to first principles could restore its force – its unique capacity both to bind society and to transform it. He was very much living in the real, modern world of the mid-nineteenth century, a world in conflict, in which battle lines were sharply drawn in terms of class and power. His purpose was to change that world through his art. This programme of Wagner's was not only far ahead of his contemporaries; it was far ahead of his own practice, as he freely acknowledged. He spoke dismissively of his earlier works, based as they were on models that he now rejected: grand opera (*Rienzi*) and German Romantic opera (*The Flying Dutchman, Tannhäuser*). *Lohengrin*, which he had still not yet heard, was a step towards something different, but it was still divided up into arias and ensembles in a way that would be abolished in the Art-work of the Future, which would, needless to say, have nothing to do with opera houses – those desecrated temples, those whorehouses of sullied art. It would need a newly built performance space, erected in a meadow, perhaps; singers and orchestra and chorus would be recruited locally; the whole thing would be free of charge. There would be three performances – no more – of *Siegfried's Death*, as he still thought of it, after which he would burn first the theatre, then the score and say to people: 'If you enjoyed it, go and do it yourself!' The whole of Wagner's idealism is contained in this vision, a vision to which he adhered to the very end; it kept him going through the long, bitter decades of struggle and setback ahead of him.

All of this was entirely new thinking. There were among Wagner's contemporaries a select few musicians whose seriousness he admired – Spontini, for example, and Berlioz – but no one, and certainly no one writing operas, had thought so deep and so hard about opera or theatre; no one had a vision of its future. Like all true radicals, he went all the way back to first principles, to the origins, both of the theatre, and of opera. His theories, with their strict rules about the relationship between words and music, echo the ideas that led to the birth of opera in the late sixteenth century, though their outcome was entirely different. When the Camerata dei Bardi in Florence set out to reconstruct Greek theatre, they started from the conviction that all Greek classical plays had been through-sung, so they slavishly adhered to the rule of one note per syllable, aspiring to a ritualistic formality of action. But their engagement with the myths was precisely that: formal, not visceral, their purpose to create harmony and exalted feeling; Wagner was attempting to undo the surface, to transcend phenomenological perceptions and engage with the reality behind reality. This was, of course, a profoundly destabilising activity, and it was meant to be. Wagner sought to bring his audiences to his own level of emotional freedom, to sweep away bourgeois inhibitions, bourgeois society's determination to live behind a mask. Art was the antidote to the discontents of civilisation: freedom was the goal.

There is a distinctly 1960s quality to Wagner's thinking around this time, which includes his thinking about being German. Back to nature – back to the good old pagan truths that have been hidden from view by Europeanism, by internationalism, by globalised values. Listen to the earth, feel your roots, man. All of which sounds pretty positive. A question inevitably arises, though: who are these people who have obscured the good old pagan truths? Who are the rootless, the foreign people who have diluted our heritage to the point where it's invisible? Who are these outsiders? Well, guess who? The Jews, of course, who seemed to be everywhere after their so-recent liberation from the ghettoes – these people with their international connections, who exist beyond nation, beyond history. Wagner started to form a theory; he had theories about everything, and he committed this particular one to a pamphlet which he called *Judaism in Music*, published some four years before *Opera and Drama*. It is an alarming performance, but an entirely characteristic one.

To his apparently genuine bewilderment, the effects of publishing the pamphlet dogged him to the end of his life. It shows him rapidly developing from the casual anti-Semitism typical of the time into a fixed intellectual position, the dark corollary of his ever-growing embrace of Germanness. It is a remarkable document which offers a vivid glimpse of how Wagner's mind worked. It is all there: the argument from false premises, the pseudo-scientific parallels, the casual offensiveness, and somewhere, behind it all, a genuine attempt to articulate something that would identify and tap the wellsprings of his own creativity. First he affects an analytical tone, then he becomes condescending, and is finally just crude. With a Hitler-like capacity for vertical take-off, he leaps from mere irrationality to hysteria, laying about him on all sides. He starts by observing with every air of reasonableness that music – the art, he says, rather curiously, which is the easiest to learn – has become increasingly colonised by Jews, but, just as they can never fully master the tongue of the country in which they happen to settle, they can do nothing more than imitate, in hollow and unconvincing fashion, its music. Now, it is self-evident, he notes, that the only art worth anything has to be rooted in its community and its culture; a Jew in Germany is, by definition, a foreigner, an alien, so even when – like Mendelssohn, for example, or Meyerbeer – they are sophisticated and cultured, they are merely posing as Germans, churning out shallow imitations of German art. Mendelssohn, having nothing to express, no roots in his adopted culture, simply hides behind forms created by Bach. This is the same Mendelssohn, incidentally, whose *Hebrides* and *A Midsummer Night's Dream* overtures and *Italian* and *Scotch* symphonies Wagner frequently conducted; the same Mendelssohn who had died just three years before Wagner wrote his pamphlet, at the age of thirty-eight, universally mourned as the outstanding musician of his age.

To Wagner he was the epitome of a 'vapid, neutered composer'. But the appearance of a Mendelssohn was merely symptomatic of the present age: in the good old days, says

Wagner, right up to the time of Mozart and Beethoven, when music had possessed what he calls 'a real organic *life-need*', the idea of a Jewish composer would have been absurd. No foreign element can become part of the life of a truly living organism. Only when a body is dying can extraneous elements become part of it, and then only to destroy it. The body's flesh then dissolves into a swarming colony of insect life, he says, active, but scarcely alive. The soul of art can only survive in living bodies, and not within what he calls its 'worm-befretted carcass'. Consciously or unconsciously, he seems to be echoing the words of Martin Luther in his savage 1543 tract *On the Jews and Their Lies*, in which he describes Jews as 'poisonous envenomed worms'. The notion of the Jews as a rotten part of the body politic which needed to be excised was enthusiastically taken up by the Nazis.

In a parting shot, he directs an envenomed dart at the poet Heine, on whose journalistic style he had consciously modelled his own, and to whom he was indebted for the plots of two of his operas, *The Flying Dutchman* and *Tannhäuser* – with whom, indeed, he had passed many convivial and stimulating evenings in Dresden. 'Whoever heard of a poetry-writing Jew,' Wagner asks, 'while Goethe and Schiller sang among us?' But when they fell silent and German poetry 'became a lie', then it was left to 'a highly gifted Jew' to expose what Wagner calls 'the bottomless aridity and Jesuitical hypocrisy of our versifying'; Heine himself attacked his famous 'musical co-religionists', mercilessly mocking them for pretending to be artists. But then, having performed this useful service, Heine convinced himself that he was a poet, and was rewarded by having his 'versified lies' set to music by German composers. Up to that point, says Wagner, Heine had been the conscience of Judaism, just as Judaism was the evil conscience of our modern civilisation. Now he was just another fraudulent pretender to the great heritage of German poetry. Wagner does not mention that he himself had made a setting of Heine's 'The Two Grenadiers'. Nor of course does he allude to a remarkably prescient letter Heine had written in 1832, warning the French of the 'demonic powers of ancient German pantheism'. One day, he said, their German neighbours, 'fired by a terrible combination of absolutist metaphysics, historical memories and resentment, fanaticism and savage strength and fury, would fall upon them, and would destroy the great monuments of Western civilisation'. In *Judaism in Music*, Wagner distils many of the elements of the lethal cocktail that Heine identifies with such unnerving precision.

No doubt he felt a great deal better after delivering himself of it. Not for long; the reaction was immediate and overwhelmingly hostile. Those closest to him were appalled. He read the essay out loud, as he read everything he wrote out loud, to Minna, who was dismayed, and told him so, accusing him of offending whole generations of people who had shown him nothing but kindness. He rewarded her for her honesty by never again reading or playing her anything he had written. The pamphlet created a wave of revulsion and animosity; soon – even though he had taken the precaution of using a Bunyanesque pseudonym: K. Freigedank – 'K. Freethought' – it threatened to engulf him. The publisher was hounded nearly to the point of ruin, and the circle of generous friends Liszt had connected to Wagner now abandoned him. He was widely criticised in the press. Commenting on his sudden unpopularity, he remarks casually in *My Life*, 'Of course, it must be remembered that almost all the newspapers in Europe were in the hands of Jews.' His attitude to Jews was increasingly pathological: it was a subject to which he reverted again and again. He appeared to be devoid of self-censorship, seemingly in the grip of a form of Asperger's syndrome, something that appeared to be beyond his control. In his calmer moments, he told many people that he disapproved of the modern anti-Semitic movement, and many of his best friends – or, more accurately, his closest musical associates – were Jewish. They were surprisingly untroubled by his venomous tirades: 'there he goes again', seemed to be their attitude. Where did it come from, all this bile? Had Jews ever done him any harm, or slighted him? On the contrary, every Jew he had ever met had bent over backwards to help him. It was entirely thanks to Meyerbeer's warm recommendation that *Rienzi* got its premiere, which firmly put him on the map just at the moment when he thought he was washed up. Heine and Mendelssohn were courteous and encouraging when he was still a young and untried composer, treating him as if he were their equal. His first girlfriend, Leah David, was Jewish.

The fact is that Wagner was unable to function, as a man or as an artist, without a sense of mission, a sense of being for something which others were – supposedly – against. Having a whole race at his disposal for that purpose was wonderfully convenient. He admits as much in a remarkable letter he wrote to Liszt shortly after the appearance of the article:

> You ask me about the anonymous article, *Judaism and Music*. You must have known that I wrote it, so why ask? For a long time now I have harboured a growing resentment against the Jews. This grudge is as necessary to my nature as gall is to blood. Their damned scribblings kept annoying me, so at last I fired with all guns blazing. It seems I have hit my target. This pleases me, for all I wanted was to terrify them a little.

Actually, as far as Wagner was concerned, his comments on Jews and music were completely subsidiary to his main point: the fact – surely incontrovertible, he felt – that German art was in decline. It needed rescuing and he was the man to do it. He was psyching himself up to the role of superhero: only when he believed he was Siegfried would he be able to liberate Brünnhilde; Jews were merely the dragon. Among other things, *Judaism in Music* was a declaration of independence, a statement of intent: he had now finally ended his long apprenticeship, using the work of others as a basis and starting point. He had found his identity, his method, which was to draw his music from inside himself, nourishing himself in his native soil, sinking deep roots into his culture. As ever, he needed to dramatise himself and his situation in the world before he could believe in it. Now, at last, he was ready to embark on his life's work.

On the most basic level, of course, his noxious little pamphlet expressed a sense of profound injustice: Meyerbeer and Mendelssohn were successful and rich, and he wasn't. His poverty during his exile and beyond it was grinding and perpetual.

And all the time, in the midst of this rackety life of scrounging and seducing, hustling and pamphleteering, his creative mind was functioning profoundly at subterranean levels; *The Ring of the Nibelung* was slowly germinating.

SEVEN

It Begins

It was a long time before he was ready to write it. Liszt, who, despite his frequent disapproval of Wagner's behaviour, was unwavering in advancing his work, secured a commission from the Grand Duke of Weimar for *Siegfried's Death*; Wagner started composing it, but gave up the attempt, he said, when he realised that there was no one who could possibly embody the Brünnhilde of his imagination. Now that Schröder-Devrient was *hors de combat*, her vocal instrument hopelessly frayed by the intense expressive demands she had made of it, there was no one else: all the female singers he knew were just fastidious schoolgirls, he said. He needed a truly heroic figure. And as he thought of these inadequate singers, and the woeful insufficiency of the stage as it was, he broke out in a painful rash all over his body. He immersed himself in hot sulphur baths, which relaxed his mood enough for him to conceive of a playful prequel to *Siegfried's Death* which would be called *Young Siegfried*. He started taking greater care of his health, giving up alcohol, tea and coffee; but, partly because of a mood of political despair induced by Louis-Napoléon's coup d'état in 1851, which seemed to him to usher back into political life all the corruption, superficiality and reaction that the 1848 revolutions had sought to abolish, he was depressed, physically and mentally, for almost a year. And then, out of the blue, on 23 May 1852, his thirty-ninth birthday, he sat down to write; in just over a month he had completed the poem-libretto for the monumental work he called *The Ring of the Nibelung*.

It now consisted of three enormous instalments, *The Valkyrie, Siegfried*, and *The Twilight of the Gods* (as he now renamed *Siegfried's Death*), telling the story of his hero, from conception to immolation. He had written the individual instalments in reverse order, discovering from each one how much further back into the story he needed to go. Then, in a totally original stroke, he added a shorter preliminary opera in one continuous act, a sort of introductory drama or prelude establishing the great themes of the cycle; this he called *The Rhinegold*. Weaving his complex sources together, he had created a sustained epic narrative derived from the Scandinavian sagas and the thirteenth-century German *Nibelungenlied* which spanned the worlds of dwarves, giants, heroes and gods, exposing the inexorably corrupting nature of power. Interwoven with this was the story of the hero who will transform the world through love – another story of redemption. Somewhat to Wagner's surprise, he said, the flawed character of Wotan, chief of the Gods, had become the central figure, though it is his demise and the demise of everything for which he stands that offers hope for the future.

The titanic work of synthesis, of establishing the narrative, of articulating the themes, to say nothing of the creation of a huge cast of characters, was a massive undertaking even before a note had been written. Now it was done. Having conquered this artistic mountain, he felt compelled to ascend a real one – the Sidelhorn, from the top of which, dazzled, he surveyed the Italian Alps, Mont Blanc and Monte Rosa stretched out before him. He had brought a bottle of champagne with him, but, once at the top, he couldn't think of anyone whose health he wanted to drink, so he brought it back down again. On he went, in the unrelaxing company of a silent guide – limping, one-eyed and possibly homicidal – through meadows and forests, across glaciers, down into valleys, across Lake Maggiore, to Lugano, where he finally rested. Friends announced that they were joining him, so he summoned Minna and together the party forged on, across the treacherous Mer de Glace, on to the Col du Géant with its unbroken wildness, then up La Flégère, all 2,595 metres of it. Descending, Minna sprained her ankle; so they went back to Zurich.

Once there, Wagner found himself still strangely restless and dissatisfied. His operas were being produced in all the smaller theatres in Germany, but he was banned from travelling to see them. Reports of the productions were not encouraging. It was now that he wrote *On the Performing of Tannhäuser*. It had always been the most problematic of his works, and he was still tinkering with it to the end of life. His guide was written because of what he described as an unexpected upsurge in demand for it. In it he states again in the strongest possible terms his conviction that his work is unlike any other that the performers will have encountered, requiring a unique approach:

> I therefore entreat the director to cast to the winds that indulgence alas! too customarily shown to operatic favourites which leaves them almost solely in the hands of the musical director. Though, in their general belittlement of Opera as a genre, people have thought fit to let a singer perpetrate any folly he pleases in his conception of a situation, because 'an opera-singer isn't an actor, you know, and one goes to the opera simply to hear the singing, not to see a play', – yet I declare that if this indulgence is applied to the present case, my work may as well be given up at once for lost.

The failure of opera houses to pay the slightest attention to his *Tannhäuser* manual scarcely surprised him. It simply confirmed him in his conviction that no conventional theatre would ever be able to do justice to the Art-work of the Future.

He now took the unprecedented step of having the finished text of *The Ring of the Nibelung* printed and distributed, then set about performing the entire libretto for small gatherings of people, all of whom reported themselves electrified. They left him, these readings, in a state of nervous exhaustion, hoarse and weary; after the first one he was so overwhelmed that he went home without saying anything to anyone. He performed them over and over, in this way creating a longing in his listeners – and himself – for him to start composing. Meanwhile, in line with his realisation in Dresden that audiences needed to be trained, quite as much as performers, he embarked on a radical and very twenty-first-century programme of education. Despite frequent offers of productions of his work from the Opera House in Zurich, he had refused, doubting its ability to do it justice. Instead he proposed that a crack band and chorus should be assembled from all over Switzerland to perform extracts from the operas in concert under his baton; earlier in the week of the concert, in a remarkable innovation, he gave readings of the relevant librettos to ensure that people knew what they were listening to. His audiences realised that they were taking part in something new, something unprecedented, especially since, seeking to make the concerts unique for their audiences, he refused to repeat them. Zurich made a great deal of the exiled composer: the local choral society gave him a diploma of honour, and a torchlight procession accompanied him home while the band played selections from his work. There were touching speeches: 'In my reply,' he wrote to Liszt, 'I saw no reason, in fact, why Zurich should not be destined, in its solid bourgeois way, to offer an impetus toward the fulfillment of my higher aims, with respect to the artistic ideas I cherished.' All very gratifying; but he was still not ready to compose.

He started on his travels again, undertaking another long and strenuous trip to Italy, this time alone. Almost immediately he fell ill with dysentery (the result, he said, of eating too many ice creams). Then he took a steamer to La Spezia; a violent headwind made his stomach worse. On land at last, he staggered into the town, only to find that his hotel was located in a particularly narrow and noisy street. After a night of fever and sleeplessness, feeling wretched, he forced himself to go for a long hilly walk in the nearby forests, then lay down to sleep, which refused to come. He fell into a half-awake state in which he felt he was sinking in water. The rushing of this water resolved itself in his brain into a musical sound, the chord of E-flat major, which kept re-echoing in broken forms, creating a sense of increasing motion; but the pure and unchanging triad of E-flat major seemed to give huge weight and substance to the water, into which he felt himself sinking ever more deeply. He awoke from his doze in terror, feeling as though the waves were rushing high above his head. Once he calmed down, he understood that he was ready to compose and immediately telegraphed Minna to prepare his study.

This ripely romantic account of the process of composition is the stuff of a New Age 'Hero's Journey' textbook, or perhaps a Hollywood biopic – the illness, the voyage across water, the epic trek into the wilderness, the inspiration rising up from the subconscious – but it appears, in all its essentials, to be true. Whether or not it is slavishly accurate is less important than that it is how Wagner chose to remember it. Self-dramatisation was his essential mode, here on an epic scale; he had to believe in himself as an artist-hero, or nothing would happen. Mere craftsmanship (of which he was perfectly capable) was not creatively productive for him. 'The stream of life, I realised, was not to flow to me from outside, but from inside.' The orchestral prelude to *The Rheingold*, the great pedal point out of which the whole subsequent epic grows, must have long lain latent within him, only now finding definitive form.

Once activated, his energy was prodigious. His five-year self-imposed silence was over. He wrote *The Rheingold*, in full score, over eight weeks without a break. Or so he said. John Deathridge and other scholars have discovered that the process was more spread out than Wagner claimed. The achievement – whether it took ten weeks, twelve or even fourteen – remains astounding. It was, perhaps, the hardest of all to compose, containing as it did – as it had to, to fulfil his newly articulated system of leading motifs, each attached to a different character or a different idea – all the thematic seeds from which the rest of the work would grow. It was like nothing else that had ever been written. Wagner strictly followed the rules he had made for himself: no chorus; not an aria, a duet or an ensemble in sight; no embellishment, no decoration; one note to a syllable; character and intention alone driving the action; the musical material exclusively derived from the motifs associated with particular characters and ideas. And it embodied with amazing dexterity, within its unbroken two-and-half-hour span, Wagner's tragic critique of modern capitalism, grounded in his understanding of Feuerbach, and channelled through figures derived from the ancient myths of the German people. A theoretical, a creative, an expressive, a dramatic, a musical, an unparalleled intellectual triumph: the Art-work of the Future. In the most literal sense, as it happens: neither Wagner nor anyone else was to hear it for twenty years.

Once *The Rheingold* was completed, he immediately began composing *The Valkyrie*, but work on it was interrupted by the old familiar need to make money. He was writing, after all, for an imaginary theatre, and imaginary theatres have no budget for commissions. In March 1855 he was lured to London by the prospect of what was then a very large sum of money: £200. The Royal Philharmonic Society invited Wagner to conduct eight concerts for them over four months, including Beethoven's Ninth Symphony, a piece the society had commissioned, it is worth remembering, only thirty years earlier. It was modern music. Wagner battled with the English weather and English musical life as best he could. The orchestra, largely composed of foreign musicians, responded enthusiastically to Wagner's injunction to them at rehearsals: 'Gentlemen, play like artists!' The concerts went exceptionally well with everyone except for the press: J. W. Davison of *The Times* was unremitting in his hostility both to Wagner's music – 'the nauseous compound he manufactures' – and his conducting. 'The more we see and hear of Herr Richard Wagner, the more we are convinced that … however extraordinary a man he may be in other things, music is not his special birthright.' He was, Davison continued, either a desperate charlatan or a self-deceived enthusiast.

Wagner immediately attributed this attitude to resentment over *Judaism in Music*, and he may not have been wrong: the pamphlet had been widely read even in England and caused almost universal revulsion. He had also refused to kowtow to Davison, who expected to be courted. In general, he was unimpressed by the English. 'Your typical Englishman is your typical sheep. They both have a practical mind which makes them find their fodder in the meadow. But they have no eyes for the beautiful meadow and the sky above. Poor me, who knows all about beautiful meadows and blue skies but can't get at the fodder.' Wagner preferred to spend time with Prosper Sainton, the naïve and fiery French leader of the orchestra, and his partner, Herr Lüders, a full-blooded German musician from Hamburg, brusque but friendly, who lived together, Wagner said, like a married couple, each tenderly concerned for the other's welfare; sex seems always to have been in the air when Wagner was about. He was notably relaxed about homosexuality, and throughout his career owed a great deal to gay enthusiasts of his work.

Despite the critical denunciation of his performances, according to which every concert he conducted was a fiasco, they were exceptionally well attended. Queen Victoria and Prince Albert attended the last but one; Albert had particularly requested the overture to *Tannhäuser*. They had an agreeable conversation afterwards, in which the prince consort lamented that Wagner's operas would never succeed in English because all the singers here were Italian, to which the queen riposted rather wittily – and accurately – that most of the Italian singers in London were in fact German. The queen told him that she was pleased to make his acquaintance. 'Just think,' Wagner wrote to Minna, 'in Germany, the police are after me and treat me like a highway robber, and the Queen of England is *pleased to make my acquaintance*.' The queen invited him to Windsor Castle, where he conducted a programme consisting of music by Spohr, Weber, and Cherubini, in addition to Mozart's *Jupiter* symphony and Beethoven's Eighth, ending with the overture to *Tannhäuser*. She was delighted, telling her diary that the overture was 'quite overpowering, so grand and in parts wild, striking and descriptive'. The royal family were a little German oasis for Wagner; for the rest he had to deal with English puritanism as best he could: he wrote a brief introduction to the Prelude to Act I of *Lohengrin*, only to find that the words 'God' and 'Holy Grail' had been deleted, leaving his audience in some confusion as to what the piece could possibly be about. For the rest, the cliques and the cabals of the music world confirmed his view that in the vauntedly free land of England, things were done pretty much as they were done everywhere else. Berlioz was in town, and they commiserated over the situation; Meyerbeer was conducting his recent *L'Etoile du Nord* at Covent Garden, which the press tumbled over itself to praise. Wagner strictly avoided opera houses during his visit, instead enjoying the boulevard theatre and such Shakespeare as he could catch.

All his impressions of London, he said, merged into a memory of almost uninterrupted ill-health, caused, he did not doubt, by the London climate. He had a perpetual cold; his friends' advice to follow a heavy English diet in order to resist the effect of the capital's polluted air did not improve matters in the least. Nor could he get his lodgings warm. His one consolation was the zoo in Regent's Park: 'the animals are magnificent'. The task he had brought with him – the orchestration of *The Valkyrie*, which he had hoped to finish off in London – only advanced a paltry hundred pages. He had left it too long since composing it, he realised, and sat for hours in front of the pencil-scrawled pages covered in meaningless hieroglyphics, which he was now incapable of deciphering. He took to reading Dante, finding the descriptions of hell in *Inferno* curiously realistic as he peered out of the window at the London fog in the middle of June.

Back in Zurich he was assailed by a particularly brutal attack of erysipelas; he blamed the English climate for that too. It stopped him from working; all he could manage in this state was reading. He immersed himself in an introduction to Buddhism, which had immediate issue in a never-finished sketch for a play about spiritual transformation called *The Victors*. Wagner was much taken with Buddhist philosophy, struck above all by the notion that to the mind of Buddha the past lives of every being appear before him as plainly as the present one. He saw at once that this had a musical implication: the continuous reminiscence in the music of this double existence, past and present, he said, would carry a powerful emotional charge. This was clearly consonant with the cumulative effect of the leitmotifs in *The Ring*: as the story progresses, the music carries with it the memory of all that has happened. But his encounter with Buddhism also found its way into the libretto he was simultaneously evolving on the subject of the Irish princess Isolde and her Cornish lover Tristan. For Wagner, the very essence of the story was contained in the Buddhist notions of the suspension of time – the eternal here and now, or *sunyata* – and the interpenetration of inner and outer worlds.

Buddhism was just one of many intellectual avenues he pursued at this time. Wagner had always longed to understand what he called the real value of philosophy. He had attended lectures on the subject in Leipzig, he had struggled with Hegel and Schelling; he had read Feuerbach, as we have seen, initially with delight, then with impatience. Philosophy somehow failed to yield its secrets to him. This frustrated him, because it was in his nature to seek underlying patterns and overarching structures; his mind, though completely untrained, was instinctively of a theorising bent. In his writings from this period he weaves and ducks his way inexpertly through history, philology, archaeology and linguistics, plucking from here and there, backtracking, going round in circles, until he reaches conclusions which provide him with a solid foundation from which at last to start work. Both his instinctively revolutionary social thinking and his newly evolved artistic theories postulated an ideal organisation of society; these were the underpinnings of the Art-work of the Future, which pointed strongly towards the creation of a new world order. However trenchant its criticism of the old order, his libretto for *The Ring of the Nibelung* was grounded in a profound optimism for mankind. But even as he was composing *The Rheingold*, which is in many ways the purest embodiment of his artistic and political theories – a narratively driven piece, in which everything is at the service of the text, which makes no concession to operatic form, and is entirely epically impersonal, sharply analysing the untenability of current social relations – his friend, the radical poet Georg Herwegh, casually tossed him an intellectual hand grenade, which almost instantly exploded his carefully constructed philosophical and political positions.

* * *

Arthur Schopenhauer was thirty when, the year after Wagner was born, he began writing the first volume of his masterpiece, *The World as Will and Presentation*; its publication in 1819 was barely noticed, nor was that of part two, published twenty-five years later. Herwegh handed Wagner the book a decade after that, in 1854, by which time it was just beginning to impinge on German intellectual life. It marks a radical break with the whole German philosophical tradition, subjecting Kant's transcendental idealism to a comprehensive overhaul, and rejecting wholesale both Hegel's dialectical materialism and Feuerbach's theory of the primacy of the senses. Schopenhauer describes the world as an illusion, and an enslaving one at that, which can only be escaped by connecting to another dimension – that of erotic love. The will, which seeks to conquer the external world, is an obstacle to connecting with this reality; the task of life, says Schopenhauer, is in fact to suspend the will. Any notion of political progress, of reshaping society, is both absurd and impossible.

These propositions – so strikingly similar to the Buddhist world view in which Wagner had recently immersed himself – are clearly in flat contradiction to the materialist philosophical position out of which Wagner's libretto for *The Ring of the Nibelung* had arisen, and to which he was still deeply committed when he started composing it. Nonetheless he found himself eagerly imbibing Schopenhauer's propositions, feeling, indeed, as if he had known them at some subconscious level all his life. The sense that life is experienced as pain, frustration, compulsion; that it is a shoddy charade; and that the only human experience that is in any sense real is sexual love, which, in its all-consuming intensity, obliterates the material world – all this was exactly how Wagner understood the world. Schopenhauer even went so far as to compare the illusory quality of human experience to a theatre performance:

the world that we perceive, as his translator Richard E. Aquila says, 'is a "presentation" of objects in the theatre of our own mind'. Wagner realised with a jolt that he had unconsciously imbued his Wotan in the Nibelung tetralogy with just the sense of inner despair that Schopenhauer describes in his great book. He read the entire massive work over and over again – four times, from beginning to end, allowing it to infuse him with its language and its world view. He was a changed man after his immersion in Schopenhauer, and longed to express himself in poetry: the serious mood created by what he had read, he said, was trying to find ecstatic expression. By chance his young friend and general musical dogsbody, Karl Ritter (another gay member of his entourage), had shown Wagner his treatment of the story of Tristan and Isolde; in it, he had focussed on the comedy of the cuckolded king. It was no laughing matter to Wagner: he saw only the tragedy in it, and immediately started writing his own poem-libretto on the subject, at the heart of which were the ideas he had absorbed from Buddhism and from Schopenhauer concerning the suspension of time and the interpenetration of inner and outer worlds. In his shaping of the material, the lovers, enemies when the opera begins, and determined to kill themselves by taking a poisoned draught, are instead given a love potion; from that moment each longs to be united in the timeless reality of death.

At the time he first read Schopenhauer's book, Wagner was at the beginning of an intense friendship with Mathilde, the beautiful wife of the young Zurich silk merchant Otto Wesendonck, who had invited the Wagners to stay with him, offering Wagner generous financial support; over two or three years Wagner's tendresse for Mathilde seems to have developed into a full-blown passion. Whether it progressed to physical consummation is impossible to know, but there is no question that Wagner had given himself over to a cauterising emotional and erotic experience. Early in his relationship with the young couple, he had written two pieces dedicated to Mathilde – the very first pieces he had written after his long sabbatical since finishing *Lohengrin* five years earlier; slight as they are, they have a certain unresolved intensity which presages the overwhelming emotions unleashed in *Tristan* three years later.

It is, however, by no means certain whether the passion preceded the work or the work preceded the passion. *Tristan and Isolde* is at least as much inspired by Schopenhauer as it is by Mathilde Wesendonck. *The World as Will and Presentation* is profoundly preoccupied with aesthetics, especially with music. At times, Wagner almost seems to be illustrating what he has read in Schopenhauer's pages, notably a passage concerning the essential tension in music, which he says is of all the arts best able to do justice to the nature of the human heart (that is, the will), which forever oscillates between satisfaction and dissatisfaction: 'The constant disunion and reconciliation of its two elements … is, metaphysically considered, a copy of the origination of new wishes, and then of their satisfaction. Thus, by flattery, music penetrates into our hearts, for it presents the image of the complete satisfaction of its wishes.' He continues with a description of musical suspension in formal and analytical terms. It is, he says, 'a dissonance which delays the final consonance'. This consonance is awaited with certainty, which only strengthens the longing for it, causing its final appearance to be all the more satisfying. This, he says, is:

> clearly an analogue of the heightened satisfaction of the will through delay. The complete cadence requires the preceding chord of the seventh on the dominant; because the most deeply felt satisfaction and the most entire relief can only follow the most earnest longing. Thus, in general, music consists of a

constant succession of more or less disquieting chords, that is, chords which excite longing, and more or less quieting and satis- fying chords; just as the life of the heart (the will) is a constant succession of greater or less disquietude through desire and aversion, and just as various degrees of relief.

This essentially sexual formulation by Schopenhauer of the effect of music on the listener – its direct visceral power of stirring the soul (or the will) – was so precisely how Wagner conceived of the way that music worked that he was, he said, 'almost stupefied' by it. The notion of delayed gratification, harmonically and in the melody itself, as an analogue of human desire, led absolutely directly to the composition of *Tristan and Isolde* – surely a unique example, as Bryan Magee suggests, of hard-core philosophical argument inspiring a specific piece of music.

It is almost impossible to do justice to the richness and complexity of Wagner's creative furor at this point in time. He was forty-three years old, was finally completing the orches- tration of *The Valkyrie* and beginning to compose *Siegfried*, while germinating *Tristan* and actively contemplating *Parsifal*. It took its toll. He was almost continuously ill throughout the composition of *The Ring*, racked with erysipelas, for which he took endless water and sulphur cures. At such times he stopped composing, on one occasion taking advantage of the interruption in his work to familiarise himself with the rudi- ments of architecture: he planned to design a house, the cost of which he hoped would be met by the sale of his scores; it wasn't, but Wagner tucked away his newly acquired knowl- edge until such time as he might have a use for it. He finally found a cure for his erysipelas – a simple water regimen, it turned out – and resumed composing; but now he was distracted by a tinker outside his house, and various amateur musicians within it, all of whom drove him mad (but provided him with the unconscionable racket of Mime's forges at work in *Siegfried*). Desperate for somewhere quiet in which to write, he tried to persuade Wesendonck to buy him a large estate: 'I gradually created in him a desire to purchase a wide tract of land,' said Wagner, in a revealing turn of phrase; in the end it cost too much even for the millionaire silk merchant, so instead he bought a nice little summer country house for Wagner's use, just over the road from the Wesendoncks' own estate.

Wagner and Minna, fighting furiously all the while, had the place refitted for all seasons, and moved in: they called it *Asyl* – asylum, a place of refuge, though with the perpetual running wars between them it must more often felt more like an asylum in its other sense. Nonetheless he continued working on *Siegfried* Act II, but then, on his forty-fourth birthday, hearing some friends singing sequences from *The Valkyrie* and *The Rheingold*, he was suddenly repulsed with the idea of continuing work on *Siegfried*. Head and heart brimming with Mathilde and with Schopenhauer, it was *Tristan and Isolde* that he wanted to write – or rather, that he needed to write; as he struggled with *Siegfried*, a quite different music was forming in his head, demanding to be written. So, in mid-scene, just before the end of Act II, when Siegfried says of Mime '*Dass der mein Vater nicht ist*' – 'this is not my Father' – he suddenly stopped writing *Siegfried*, scribbling on the score 'When shall we meet again? RW'. In fact, he could not forbear from leaving Act II just hanging, so he finished it a few days later, but did not come back to the score for a full twelve years. That is *artus interruptus* on a titanic scale.

EIGHT

Suspension

Wagner being Wagner, his motives for embarking on *Tristan* were neither purely artistic nor exclusively erotic: he had a commercial motive too. He knew that no regular opera house could contemplate staging *The Ring*, nor indeed did he want one to; only a theatre expressly designed by him could do it justice. Meanwhile, he needed to make money, so an opera with a small cast and simple scenic needs might be a sensible, saleable proposition. Since he was still banned from the German Confederation, he thought of doing it perhaps in Strasbourg, or even Brazil. When an old colleague, now working for the Duke of Baden, suggested that he might do it there, Wagner immediately set to work full time on the libretto. He wrote no music. Before starting on *The Rhinegold* he had written a simple little polka for Mathilde Wesendonck, followed by a rather more feeling piano sonata, his second: it is the best of his piano pieces. But in November 1857, as a sort of warm-up for *Tristan*, and no doubt to flatter Mathilde, he set three Schopenhauerian poems she had written.

The second of the poems, 'Stand Still!' suggests the extraordinary intensity between them:

> Roaring and rushing wheel of time,
> You are the measurer of Eternity;
> Shining spheres in the wide universe,
> You who surround the world globe,
> Eternal creation, halt!
> Enough development, let me be!

Cease, generative powers,
The primal thoughts which you are ever creating!
Slow your breathing, still your urge
Silently, only for a second long!
Swelling pulses, fetter your beating,
End, o eternal day of willing!
That in blessed, sweet forgetfulness,
I may measure all my bliss!

When one eye another drinks in bliss,
And one soul into another sinks,
One nature in another finds itself again,
And when each hope's fulfilment is finished,
When the lips are mute in astounded silence,
And no wish more does the heart invent,
Then man recognises the sign of Eternity,
And solves your riddle, holy Nature!

He set two more of Mathilde's poems, explicitly designated studies for *Tristan*, quoting the score of the opera itself – or perhaps it is the score which quotes the songs. It is music pregnant with yearning and unresolved emotional complexity – music, supremely, of suspension. Now he and Mathilde were indissolubly bound together in art. Wagner made a luscious transcription of one of the songs, 'Träume', for violin and small orchestra, which he conducted with a group of Zurich musicians under Mathilde's bedroom window on her birthday, in December 1857; Minna no doubt watching it all, remarks Wagner's biographer Ernest Newman, 'as suspiciously as Melot watched the lovers in the opera'. Unconsummated the relationship may have been, but it powerfully fed his imagination. 'As I have never in life felt the real bliss of love,' he wrote to Liszt, 'I must erect a monument to the most beautiful of all my dreams, in which, from beginning to end, that love shall be thoroughly satiated. I have in my head *Tristan and Isolde*, the most full-blooded musical conception.'

The moment he finished the text of *Tristan*, he gave Mathilde first sight of it, and then, shortly after, as was his wont, he read it out loud for a small group of intimates, consisting of Minna, the Wesendoncks, Liszt's twenty-year-old daughter Cosima, and her new husband, the virtuoso pianist and conductor Hans von Bülow. Wagner had known both Cosima and Hans since they were very young. Cosima he had first met at her father's house in Paris when she was 'an anxious, ugly child'; Wagner entertained her and the other children by reading them the libretto of *The Ring*. None of them spoke a word of German, but he held them all gripped, none more so than Cosima. As for Hans, Wagner had met him in Dresden when the boy was sixteen and been astonished by his pianistic prowess. Bülow later became a pupil of Liszt, giving the first public performance of the Piano Sonata in B minor; and it was hearing Liszt conduct the first performance of *Lohengrin* in Weimar that had decided the young man to give up the law, in defiance of his parents, and become a professional musician. Wagner himself even wrote to Bülow's parents, urging them to let him follow this course.

So everyone in the little audience who heard him read the *Tristan* libretto with his customary brilliance and emotional force had a strong personal investment in him. Each of them, in different ways and for different reasons, was visibly shaken by the story of overwhelming adulterous sexual passion, especially the three women: his past, his present and his future. Wesendonck no doubt had suspicions about Wagner's relationship with Mathilde, though he said nothing. Mathilde herself was dreadfully upset by the last act, with both lovers dead; Wagner cheered her up by telling her that things normally ended up that way in 'those sort of stories'. Cosima sat silent with her head bowed; when pressed for an opinion, she began to cry. If Minna said anything, it was not reported, but she knew in her gut that something was going on; the songs Wagner had written for Mathilde can only have confirmed her suspicions – he certainly wasn't writing songs like that for her.

Aware of the manifold tensions in Zurich, Wagner slipped off to Paris, for inconclusive talks about a potential production of *Tannhäuser*. He was in need of a piano, and he knew just how to get it. 'I say, Franz,' he wrote to Liszt, with whom he had a voluminous correspondence, largely taken up with the ways in which Liszt could be of assistance to him, 'I've just had a divine idea. YOU MUST GET ME AN ERARD GRAND!':

> Write to the widow and tell her that you visit me THREE TIMES every year, and that you must absolutely have a better grand piano than the old and lame one in my possession. Tell her a hundred thousand fibs, and make her believe that it is for her a point of honour that an Erard should stand in my house. In brief, do not think, but act with the impudence of genius. I MUST HAVE AN ERARD. If they will not give me one let them lend me one on a yard-long lease.

The phrase 'impudence of genius' must have struck Liszt with some irony. Wagner had discovered that when that great man, now more renowned as a conductor and an increasingly influential composer than as a pianist, recognised exceptional gifts in a fellow musician, he felt compelled to advance that person, even if, as was the case with Wagner, his demands were exorbitant. He must have prevailed on *la veuve Erard*, because when Wagner met her, she did indeed offer him a piano, which was duly shipped to Switzerland, and from then on followed him wherever he went, battered from without by travel and from within by his savage assaults on the keyboard.

Back in Zurich, at that same piano, he started work – vaguely, he said, and somewhat hopelessly – on the score of *Tristan*. He finished the first act in a little over three months and despatched it to the engraver; to mark the event he sent a pencil sketch of one of the themes to Mathilde with a rather steamy note: 'Everything seems so indisputably true to me, and I am so sure of myself,' he wrote, 'whenever your wonderful, sacred eyes rest upon me, and I sink into them. Then there are no more objects and subjects; then everything is one and the same, deep and immeasurable harmony! Today I'll be in the garden, and I hope to find a moment alone with you.' He signed off: 'Take my entire soul for a morning's greeting!' Minna intercepted the letter, with predictable consequences. She was quite incapable, Wagner said when she confronted him with it, of understanding the state of mind he had described in the letter, so she gave it what he called 'a vulgar interpretation'. He advised her not to take the matter any further, but she did, marching over to the Wesendoncks and confronting them with her suspicions – 'doing', as she told Wagner, 'what any wise woman would do'. He immediately packed her off early to a spa she had been booked into; the Wesendoncks, meanwhile, banned her from their house. Minna delivered a parting shot to her rival: 'I must tell you with a bleeding heart that you have succeeded in separating my husband from me after nearly twenty-two years of marriage. May this noble deed contribute to your peace of mind, to your happiness.' In this poisoned atmosphere, Wagner sat down at his new Erard piano, and seemed, he said, to drift quite naturally into the nocturnal sound world of Act II of *Tristan*.

It was clearly time to leave Zurich. When Minna returned from the spa, Wagner immediately banished her back home to her parents in Saxony, but not before she had enraged him all over again by taking an advertisement in the local papers offering their domestic effects at cut prices 'owing to sudden departure'. The Wesendoncks left town at the same time, and Wagner set off for Italy – for Venice, which was under Austrian rule, but Austria was a relatively relaxed member of the German Confederation, so Wagner felt safe from arrest there. Nonetheless, the sombre spectacle of the gondolas with their black awnings filled him with premonitions: he felt, he said, that he was taking part in a funeral procession during a pestilence. It proved hard for him to dispel the melancholy which seemed to envelop the city. The police kept a watchful though distinctly benevolent eye on him: they were rather excited to have such a celebrity in their midst, 'the central figure of the new musical movement', as the chief of police describes him in a despatch, 'the begetter of the so-called "music of the future"'. The report continues, 'as a proof of the overwrought state of his nerves, we may mention that on the day of his arrival at the Palazzo Giustiniani he asked his landlord's permission to change the wallpaper of his apartment, which was too red for his taste, and the very next day he had the rooms repapered'. He sent for his Erard and his bed; he avoided the social and musical life of the city – though he was not displeased to be regaled by passing brass bands bashing out the overtures to *Rienzi* and *Tannhäuser* – and set to work on the second act of *Tristan*, in which the lovers are united in their timeless ecstasy, sunk in deepest night, until discovered by Tristan's liege, King Mark. Despite enduring an agonising carbuncle on his leg, and receiving intimations that the Saxon court was applying pressure on the Venetian authorities for him to be extradited, Wagner lingered in Venice through the whole of the winter, alone and rootless. War between France and Piedmont made the situation more and more unstable; troops flooded the streets. The officers made a pleasant impression on him; less so the conscripted rank and file, cursed as they were with what he called the 'dull servile features' of certain Slav countries within the Austrian Empire. He headed off back to safe, racially pure Switzerland, to Lucerne; the Erard was sent ahead, by way of the snowbound Gotthard mountain pass, until finally it arrived at the Schweizerhof Hotel and he could begin working again. He felt, he said, like the goddess Leto, roaming the world, heavily pregnant, trying to find a place in which to give birth to Zeus's children.

Throughout 1859 he worked on Act III of *Tristan* with an engulfing sense of sadness. He could not banish from his mind the long-drawn-out wail of the *gondolieri* he had heard in Venice at night, and he wove it into the score; death-haunted Venice permeates every death-haunted bar of *Tristan*. At length he finished, and immediately turned his attention again to making some desperately needed money. That meant Paris, still the musical centre of the world. He staged a series of concerts there to introduce his work to the French public. They succeeded brilliantly with audiences, who seemed surprised, he said, that his music contained tunes; but the management had neglected to invite the critics, who then attacked him anyway. Nonetheless, for the first time he began to gather a significant fan base in Paris, including the poet Baudelaire, whose rapturous response to the concerts acknowledged, in entirely non-technical terms, the fact that Wagner's music was something quite new: 'I had a feeling of pride and joy in understanding, in being possessed, in being over-whelmed,' he wrote. 'It is a truly sensual pleasure, like that of rising in the air.' A striking feature of the response to Wagner's music is that it often spoke more vividly to writers than to musicians. 'A literary man can succeed in understanding Wagner,' remarked the Parisian journalist and novelist, 'Willy', some years later, 'but a musician, never!' Failed by his manager, Wagner took to promoting himself, something at which he had always been a dab hand. He started holding a weekly salon in his little villa in the rue d'Aumale in the 9th arrondissement; everyone who was anyone was to be found there, including the young Camille Saint-Saëns, who astounded Wagner by sight-reading *Lohengrin*, *Tannhäuser*, and *Tristan*, on which the ink was barely dry. But all that ever came of the salon were yet more debts.

Wagner's main efforts were directed towards securing a production of *Tannhäuser*; finally, thanks to the influence of Princess Metternich, the Austrian ambassador's wife, the Emperor, Napoleon III himself, commanded a performance of it at the Opéra. Wagner heartily despised the self-crowned emperor, the former President Louis-Napoléon Bonaparte, who had seized power in a ruthless coup d'état, but a production was a production, and he bit his lip. Before he had time to rejoice at the news, however, he was firmly instructed that for the piece to succeed, it was essential that he should introduce a ballet at the end of Act II: that was the point in the evening at which the members of the famous Jockey Club liked to come to the theatre to see their girlfriends in the *corps de ballet* flashing their legs and hopping about a bit, after which they would take them out on the town. Wagner's desire for a success in Paris was very great, but the final scene of Act II in *Tannhäuser* is the one in which the anguished hero repents his sins and vows to go to Rome to seek forgiveness; even Wagner's all-encompassing imagination was stumped by the challenge of creating a ballet out of that. He thought he had a solution, however. Anticipating the situation, Wagner had ingeniously extended the opera's opening sequence on the Venusberg to incorporate a bacchanalian orgy. This concession was a matter of supreme indifference to the members of the Jockey Club: they would rather have died than attend the beginning of an opera – that was when they took supper. Furthermore, Wagner was informed, the best dancers in the company would not be available to dance in the first act; at that point in the evening all the company could offer – *desolé!* – were three Hungarian peasant dancers. There was, moreover, no costume budget for the scene.

Nevertheless, despite this apparent impasse, things proceeded efficiently enough, Venusberg bacchanale and all. Wagner attended rehearsals, though he proved a somewhat disconcerting presence. 'What a devil of a man!' remarked the ballet master, Lucien Petipa, who arranged the bacchanale. 'When he wanted to come down to the orchestra pit to make remarks to the artists, instead of taking the aisles, he would step over the seats, walking as much on his hands as on his feet, and risking breaking both arms and legs.' Generally, he kept himself to himself, though what he saw often frustrated him. Apparently the only rehearsal technique known either to the director or to the conductor was simply to do it over and over again, with the result that the company became deeply dispirited; needless to say, no one had read *On the Performing of Tannhäuser*, and there were most certainly no textual analysis sessions, though the young singers Wagner had cast were lively and enthusiastic and engaged vividly with the words (it was sung in French, of course). Albert Niemann, the excellent German tenor (also very young) imported to sing the title role, was less sanguine: he had given a number of interviews to local journalists who had assured him that with no stars in the cast it would be a flop. Niemann sank into despair, cutting more and more of his role, reasoning that the sooner the inevitable catastrophe was over, the better. As for the orchestra, it proved impossible to get the ten horns called for in the first act, so Wagner found himself dealing with 'that terrible man', Adolphe Saxe, who tried to fob him off with a variety of saxhorns and saxophones. The crucial problem was that the conductor, Pierre-Louis Dietsch – the same Pierre-Louis Dietsch who had written *Le Vaisseau fantôme* more or less inspired by Wagner's scenario fifteen years earlier – was entirely unable to maintain any given tempo, with the result that the musical performance constantly fell apart; Wagner offered to take over, which predictably provoked a mutiny among the players. A message came to the composer from the emperor himself, suggesting that if he wanted a success he would be well advised to give up his pernickety demands. Eventually he resigned himself to the situation, and went to the first night with his friends, determined simply to enjoy it for what it was. At this point he discovered that he had not been allocated any tickets, so his friends all went home. The performance was a predictable shambles at every level. Nonetheless, and despite a certain amount of prearranged barracking, a few discerning members of the audience were gripped by the fervour and originality of the piece; over the evening the house began to warm to it, till by the end they were cheering.

Minna came to Paris for the second performance, sitting with Wagner and Princess Metternich. There was more barracking; at one point Minna, identified as the composer's wife, was attacked by some members of the audience, until the Wagners' faithful servant girl silenced them with a resounding *Schweinhund!* In general, though, the performance went much better than it had on the first night, with the audience genuinely rapt during Act II – until, that is, the sublime final scene, when the Landgrave commands Tannhäuser to travel to Rome with the pilgrims and ask absolution from the pope:

> At the sublime festival of clemency and grace
> I will atone for my sin in humility

sing the younger pilgrims, filled with humility and hope:

> Blessed is he who truly believes!
> He shall be saved through penitence and repentance.

At this moment, the Jockey Club made its entrance in full cry and official garb, whooping out hunting cries and playing penny whistles, and demanding their ballet. They managed to stop the performance for a full ten minutes; it never recovered. An appeal to the emperor to control them at subsequent performances failed when it turned out that most of the Jockeys were in fact members of the royal household; at the third performance the police made an appearance, but they had come, it transpired, to protect, not the public or the performers, but the *soi-disant* Jockeys. The press, which Wagner insisted was entirely under the control of Meyerbeer, was hostile, but he was encouraged by the support of the smaller journals – 'of which Meyerbeer', he darkly observed, 'had as yet taken no account'. In the circumstances, and given the uncontrollability of the Jockey Club, Wagner withdrew *Tannhäuser*, to the dismay of the management, who insisted that it had been a triumph. Various later attempts were made to revive it in Paris; one certifiably optimistic entrepreneur tried to start a 'Théâtre Wagner'. None of these schemes prevailed; for Wagner, Paris yet again proved itself to be the boulevard of broken dreams.

NINE

Limbo

Despite these reverses, things suddenly seemed to be looking up for Wagner at the end of 1861. After twelve years, the warrant for his arrest was at last rescinded. He had never lacked influential and high-powered supporters and their sustained lobbying on his behalf finally paid off: he was now once again at liberty to travel throughout the states of the German Confederation – all of them, that is, except the one in which he was born, Saxony. His exile had lasted a quarter of his entire life – during which time he had never had a place he could call his own. The man whose whole purpose in life was, as he saw it, to honour the German soul was now finally readmitted to his own country. He was not as pleased as might have been expected. 'I feel terrified when I think of Germany and my future enterprises there,' he wrote to Liszt. 'God forgive me! I can see nothing there but miserable pettiness, a mere show and boast of sterling worth, without any real founda-tion, everything and everybody half finished. I must confess that my return to German soil did not make the slightest impression on me. Believe me, we have no real country! And if I am a German,' he added, tellingly, 'I carry my Germany in my heart.' It was the idea of Germany, of Germanness, that inspired him, not the vulgar, tedious reality.

As he predicted, freedom of movement did not bring any immediate material gains. He constantly hustled from pillar to post, trying to secure productions and failing. The first thing he did was to approach the new Grand Duke of Baden, Friedrich I, to try to reanimate a formerly scheduled production of *Tristan and Isolde* which had been unaccountably shelved. The duke agreed to reschedule it, duly authorising him to contract the best singers from Vienna, but the theatre there refused to release their artists, offering instead to mount the opera themselves; the duke graciously acceded. Wagner went back to Paris to wind up his affairs there, among them his marriage. The dog Peps had died, and with it, Wagner thought, the last remnants of the relationship. He promised to provide Minna with 3,000 marks a year for the rest of her life; she accepted the inevitability of the situation and traipsed sadly back to Dresden. Wagner went to Weimar, where Liszt ensured that he was received like a conquering hero, then on to Vienna for *Tristan*. But in Vienna the Tristan was ill with some nameless vocal condition; rehearsals proceeded, tenorlessly, in a desultory sort of way. At this point, the orchestra insisted that the score was unplayable. Despairing, Wagner escaped to Venice, where so much of the opera had been conceived and written; he was the guest of the Wesendoncks, who had now put the little upset precipitated by Minna behind them. Venice did nothing to cheer his spirits, until one day Wesendonck took him to the Gallerie dell'Accademia, where he saw Titian's explosive altarpiece, *The Assumption of the Virgin*, which so stimulated him that his old creative energies revived, as though in a sudden electric flash of inspiration, and he at once determined to go back to the libretto for *The Mastersingers of Nuremberg* he had sketched out sixteen years earlier. All it had taken to reanimate his divine afflatus was an injection of art.

This is where Wagner becomes almost incomprehensible to mere mortals. His domestic affairs in tatters; the Paris production of *Tannhäuser*, on which he had pinned such high hopes, a spectacular disaster; *Tristan and Isolde*, *The Rheingold*, *The Valkyrie* and two thirds of *Siegfried* complete but unperformed – and he embarks on yet another massive project with no prospect whatever of a production. For a confirmed pessimist he seems to have had astonishing reserves of optimism – or perhaps simply a blind belief in himself and his mission. 'I know what I'll do!' he seems to say to himself when things are going particularly badly, 'I'll write a four-and-a-half-hour opera!' The next day he was on the carriage back to Vienna to drop in on rehearsals for *Tristan*; on the journey, he says, the entire overture to *The Mastersingers* came to him. Still of no fixed abode, and penniless, he then set off for Paris. Why? He had known only humiliation there. He had been hoping to stay with Princess Metternich at the Austrian embassy, but that proved impossible, for typically Wagnerian reasons: the princess's father-in-law, a dangerous Hungarian lunatic, had to be kept under armed guard twenty-four hours a day and the only place where that was possible was the embassy; clearly there was only room there for one lunatic at a time, so Wagner had to find lodgings for himself. Wherever he went, whatever he did, Wagner seemed to encounter or possibly to create extraordinary and volatile situations: if he went up a mountain, the guide was inevitably one-eyed, malevolent and in touch with the spirit world; if he sat at an outdoor table in an ordinary *Weinstube*, a flock of thirty birds would immediately descend from the skies and share his sandwich with him. He was in a state of constant self-dramatisation and the universe around him seemed only too willing to connive in the process. The results were not normally benign: 'Every man has his daemon, and mine is a frightful monster,' he admitted to a friend. 'When he is hovering about me a catastrophe is in the air. The only time I have ever been on the sea I was nearly shipwrecked; and if I were to go to America, I am sure I should be met with a cyclone.' By those standards, the Hungarian lunatic was a minor inconvenience.

So here he was, yet again, adrift in Paris. Denied a bed at the embassy, he holed himself up with his Erard in a third-floor room in a little hotel on the Quai Voltaire, from which he surveyed the crowds teeming over the bridges and the quays, revelling in a prospect which embraced the Tuileries, the Louvre and the Hôtel de Ville. There, close to the epicentre of Paris, he wrote the libretto of the most locally German of all his operas. He had a breeze writing it; new tunes kept coming to him as he strolled whistling down the boulevards. On the other hand, he found himself cold-shouldered by pretty well everyone he'd ever known in Paris; so after a couple of months he left. Still desperate for somewhere to live free of charge, he went the rounds of the many people who had fulsomely invited him to stay with them, but drew a blank. He was rather taken aback, having assumed that in inviting himself he had been conferring an honour on them. When he sued for favours, he had two modes: one, grovelling, the other haughty. 'My dear Hornstein,' he writes to one such individual in an approach which, if scarcely ingratiating, is at least to the point:

I hear that you have become rich. In what a wretched state I myself am you can readily guess from my failures. In order to make possible this way to my preservation – that is to say, to lift me above the most distressing obligations, cares, and needs that rob me of all freedom of mind – I require an immediate loan of ten thousand francs. With this I can again put my life in order, and again do productive work. It will be rather hard for you to provide me with this sum; but it will be possible if you WISH it, and do not shrink from a sacrifice.

Hornstein, bewildered rather than offended, replied:

Dear Herr Wagner You seem to have a false idea of my riches. I have a modest fortune on which I can live in a plain and decent style with my wife and child. You must therefore turn to really rich people, of whom you have plenty among your patrons and patronesses all over Europe. I regret that I cannot be of service to you. As for your long visit to 'one of my estates', at present I cannot contrive a long visit; if it should become possible later, I will let you know.

This provoked a sharp reproof from Wagner:

Dear Herr von Hornstein It would be wrong of me to pass over without censure an answer such as you have given me. Though it will probably not happen again that a man like me will apply to you, yet a perception of the impropriety of your letter ought of itself to be a good thing for you. You should not have presumed to advise me in any way, even as to who is really rich; and you should have left it to myself to decide why I do not apply to the patrons and patronesses to whom you refer. If you are not prepared to have me at one of your estates, you could have seized the signal opportunity I offered you of making the necessary arrangements for receiving me in some place of my choice. It is consequently offensive of you to say that you will let me know whenever you will be prepared to have me.

Hornstein's commiseration at the latest cancellation of the premiere of *Tristan* is roughly brushed aside: 'You should have omitted the wish you express with regard to *Tristan*; your answer could only pass muster on the assumption that you are totally ignorant of my works. Let this end the matter. I reckon on your discretion, as you can on mine.' Astonishingly – and this gives some measure of the force of Wagner's personality – he and Hornstein remained on friendly terms.

He thought again of Baden, where he had once had a very sympathetic reception, and was granted an interview with Grand Duke Friedrich. Wagner was struck, he said with elaborate irony, by the sympathetic concern of the duke as to how he could meet the cost of his arduous life, or even his travelling expenses (questions which Wagner often asked himself).

Wagner replied that he had an advance from his publisher. On hearing this, the duke was much reassured; neither the money nor the position Wagner was angling for materialised. He worked his way round the German Confederation, passing from duke to duke, trying to secure himself a place in which to write; nothing came of it. He was baffled. His needs were so simple: a view of the Rhine, preferably from a medieval tower; a large garden; space for the Erard. Until something which met his specifications turned up, he lived in temporary accommodation in the unremarkable little town of Biebrich in Wiesbaden, where Minna joined him for 'ten days of hell', as he put it. After she'd gone, the Wesendoncks came to visit and commissioned a portrait of him from Cäsar Willich, like Wagner, a suspected revolutionary recently granted amnesty. The Bülows visited, too; Cosima read to Wagner while he was being painted. The result is a rather waxy daub, giving little indication of his vitality, but Wagner liked it well enough to have a copy made for Minna. Thus the strange vexed triangle connecting him to Mathilde, Minna and Cosima was re-established. Nothing in his personal life was simple.

Wagner's professional life was no less vexing. Friedrich of Baden offered him a production of *Lohengrin*, to be supervised by Wagner personally; the great tenor Ludwig Schnorr von Carolsfeld would sing the title role. This excellent offer was somewhat undermined by his having to deal with one his great *bêtes noires*, the theatre director, Eduard Devrient, whom he had once admired, but now demonised as the most pernicious of malevolent mediocrities. So frustrated was Wagner by Devrient's manoeuvres, which included insisting on large cuts in the score, that he went to the grand duke and withdrew the opera; Devrient had the satisfaction of being able to report to Wagner that the duke – who, Devrient said, possessed the remarkable gift of being able to distinguish the art from the artist – had graciously proposed that Wagner should nevertheless be allowed to conduct a concert of his work. Wagner refused; the art and the artist, he proudly insisted, were indivisibly one. But now Baden was off the list for possible productions.

Progress on *Mastersingers* was delayed by Wagner's failure to find a suitable place to write, by his being bitten by a dog, which put his right thumb out of action (this greatly upset him: all dogs loved him, he firmly believed), and by the growing intensity of his relationship with Cosima von Bülow, whose marriage to the increasingly irascible and depressed Hans was becoming daily more strained. One day, when they were all together, Wagner was singing – as was his wont – Wotan's fathomlessly complex farewell to Brünnhilde from the last act of the still unproduced *Valkyrie*, accompanying himself on the piano. As he sang the sublime phrases in which the father takes his leave forever from his best-beloved daughter –

> Farewell, you bold,
> wonderful child!
> You, my heart's
> holiest pride.
> Farewell, farewell, farewell!

– he noticed on Cosima's face an expression he had seen once before, in Zurich, after the reading of *Tristan*. Everything connected with her expression, he said, was shrouded in silence and mystery, but the conviction that, as he put it, 'she belonged to me', grew to such certainty in his mind that he became quite giddy with joy.

Meanwhile, *Tristan* was finally announced in Vienna, but it was some way off. Money had to be made, so *Mastersingers* was shelved again, while he conducted *Lohengrin* in Frankfurt. Wagner went from there to Leipzig – back home at last, though it may not have felt very much like it. Saxony was the last state in the confederation to rescind the order for his arrest. He received an initially frosty response from the orchestra, but they warmed up once the music-making got under way. He then went on to Dresden, where Minna had set up house; the city seemed frightfully dull, he wickedly noted, without the barricades. All his old colleagues had gone, retired or dead; he had hated most of them, anyway. The officials of the ministry of the interior, who had signed his amnesty, were still deeply suspicious of him, and there was considerable scepticism about his protestations of innocence and youthful foolishness at the time of the uprising: during his more than a decade of exile they had amassed a substantial amount of highly incriminating evidence about his activities – the guns and the hand grenades he had distributed were real and death-dealing. The events of '49 would come back to haunt him before another decade was out. While he was in Dresden, he had a dalliance with a young actress called Friederike Mayer, but even that proved problematic; eventually he packed her off to Venice, himself heading for Vienna and *Tristan*.

Once there Wagner did a remarkable thing: he arranged concerts of some of the orchestral music he had written during the years he'd been away, music neither he nor anyone else had ever heard played – from *Rhinegold*, *The Valkyrie*, *Siegfried*, *Tristan* and the overture to *The Mastersingers*, an astounding hoard of unheard masterpieces, most of which would become standard repertory items. For the Viennese it must have been like stumbling into an Aladdin's cave of undreamed-of riches. To get the concerts together, he needed an army of copyists and proof-readers, which he chose from among the young musicians who always attached themselves to him; among them on this occasion was, astonishingly, Johannes Brahms, the monumental First Piano Concerto and a great deal of masterly piano and chamber music already under his belt. 'Brahms's behaviour proved unassuming and good-natured,'

TEN

Enter a Swan

Eckert received Wagner warmly enough in Stuttgart, but there was little he could do for him beyond giving him a meal and a drink and a sympathetic ear. While they were chewing the fat over supper, a messenger came into the restaurant and presented Wagner with a card marked 'Secretary to the King of Bavaria'. Wagner immediately assumed it was from a creditor, so he sent the man off, making a furtive getaway as soon as possible. When he got back to his hotel, he found that the man had followed him. Fearing the worst, Wagner made an appointment to meet him the following morning. When they met it turned out that the man, Franz von Pfistermeister, stiff and formal in his court uniform, was indeed secretary to the newly crowned King of Bavaria, Ludwig II, who was all of eighteen years of age, his father, King Maximilian, having died suddenly at the age of fifty-three, after a three-day illness.

One of the first actions of the young king was to send Pfistermeister to find Wagner. From that point on events took on the character of a late Shakespeare romance. The elderly courtier had found the composer after an epic quest across several kingdoms and countries, going first to Vienna, then to Mariafeld in Zurich, finally locating him in Stuttgart. With due formality, the royal secretary handed Wagner a ring and a photograph from the strikingly handsome young monarch, with an accompanying letter, in which it transpired that His Majesty was greatly partial to Wagner's work and sought to advance it in every way he could. Everything Wagner needed would be provided for him in Munich, where the king very much hoped that *The Ring of the Nibelung* would be staged. The king wished to keep Wagner near him as his friend, the letter concluded, so that he might protect him from any malignant stroke of fate. Perfectly understandably, on reading the letter, Wagner cried. As if to set a symbolic seal on his triumph, while he and his Stuttgart chums were celebrating this astounding turn of events at supper that evening, news came that Giacomo Meyerbeer had just died.

Wagner knew better than most how to recognise the intervention of fate. At the end of the introduction to the published version of the *Ring* librettos, he had written: 'Will there ever come a Prince who could provide the resources necessary to bring this vast work to the stage?' But even he could scarcely have contrived such a sequence of events: to have met at his absolute lowest, with five massive unperformed operas in his bag, no prospect of productions, sub-zero credit rating, a poisonous reputation among managements, friends and, particularly, husbands – to have met at that point, not just a rich patron but a fabulously wealthy young king, one who, moreover, as Wagner would soon discover, had been obsessed by him since the age of twelve, who had memorised the texts of his all operas, even the unperformed ones, who had read and digested the longest and most intractable of his treatises, who knew all the German myths and sagas by heart, who identified personally with Lohengrin, and more particularly with the swan that bears Lohengrin, pictures of which had adorned his nursery walls when he was a baby, who was a natural hero-worshipper – to have met just that person at just that moment would only, of course, have confirmed everything Wagner believed about his destiny.

He knew exactly how to respond to the opportunity that confronted him. He sat down and dashed off a letter:

Dear, Gracious King

These tears of heavenly emotion I send to you tell you that now the marvel of poetry has come as a divine reality into my poor, love-thirsty life! And that this life, until its final outpouring of poetry and music, belongs now to you my gracious young King: dispose of it as you would your own property!

In the utmost ecstasy, faithful and true,

Your obedient Richard Wagner

The heraldic language might have come from the mouth of one of his own characters; the master touch is the phrase 'love-thirsty', an unerring description, not of himself, but of the letter's addressee. Wagner settled his hotel bill by handing over a snuff box he'd been given by some Russian grand duke, borrowed the fare for a railway ticket (first-class) to Munich, and took the next step on the dangerous road along which, as he put it, fate beckoned him to such great ends.

The following day, Wagner and Ludwig met for the first time; the relationship started at a level of intensity which it never entirely lost. Ludwig had first seen *Lohengrin* at the age of fifteen; he read *Opera and Drama* at sixteen, then worked his way through all the rest of the prose. *Tannhäuser* he first saw when he was seventeen. Wagner and everything Wagner had wrought filled his every waking minute. So to see the source of all this wonder standing before him was overwhelming. For Wagner, it was as if his lifelong dream of the artist's place in the scheme of things had at last become a reality. The diminutive composer bowed low over the immensely tall king's hand and remained a long time in that position without saying a word. 'I felt as if we had exchanged roles,' wrote Ludwig. 'I stooped down to him and pressed him to my heart, feeling that I was speaking a formal oath to myself: to remain loyal to him all my life.' The meeting was, Wagner said, like one great love scene; it seemed as though it would never end.

Ludwig showed the deepest understanding, Wagner said, of his nature and his needs: the king promised to give him everything he required in order to live; he would enable him to create and stage his own works, with no formal appointment or any duties to fulfil. 'And for this to have happened now –' cried Wagner, 'now – in the blackest night of death in my whole existence!' The entire encounter, both verbally and in its long-drawn-out intensity, might have been an extract from the still-unperformed love duet from *Tristan and Isolde*. Ludwig had (severely repressed) homosexual inclinations, but it is hard to believe that the tall, slim, charismatic youth desired the fifty-year-old hunched little composer with his huge head and popping eyes. It is rather Wagner, with his odd sensual ambivalence, who seems aroused: 'You can have no idea of the magic of his eyes!' he wrote to a friend. He feared that with his youth, beauty, soul and splendour, 'his life must run away like a fleeting, heavenly dream in this common world ... he is the one we were waiting for and whose existence was never in doubt, but it fills me with awestruck admiration to find him so fair of form'. It is the language of the fairy tale. Or myth: Wagnerian myth. 'If I am Wotan,' said Wagner, 'he is Siegfried.' He later came to refer suggestively to Ludwig as Parzival, the sacred fool who heals the world. For his part, Ludwig immediately ordered a portrait and a bust of Wagner to place alongside the ones he already had of Beethoven and Shakespeare. At last Wagner's life and his work were in step with each other. At last, the world was taking him at his own valuation. Or so it seemed.

For the time being, the fairy tale continued: by a wave of the Bavarian treasury's wand, Wagner's Viennese debts were wiped out in an instant, and he was awarded a handsome annual salary of 4,000 florins; the king bought the as yet incomplete *Ring of the Nibelung* for 30,000 florins (Otto Wesendonck had already bought the rights some years earlier, but now graciously waived them in favour of the king); Wagner was installed in a three-storey house on Lake Starnberg. Ludwig was staying nearby in Berg Castle, and Wagner was taken there every day in a royal carriage, so that Ludwig might delve deep into his soul. Wagner took this very seriously. He had met a psychic who told him it was his duty to look after Ludwig. 'The fate of this wonderful, unique youth, who is profoundly linked with me by a mystical magic, is entrusted to me, *me* … the profound meaning of my duty to the King, which is of significance to the whole people, nay to Germany itself, has been revealed to me by an almost supernatural experience.' In their sessions together, it wasn't Wagner's music or his theories they discussed: he instructed Ludwig in his sacred duties as a king. As Ludwig well knew from Wagner's pseudo-historical essay 'The Wibelungs', written in the revolutionary year of 1848, he had traced the lineage of the Germany monarchy back to the Frankish kings, 'the oldest lawful race of Kings in all the world', which had issued, according to Wagner, from a son of God 'called by his nearest kinsmen Siegfried but *Christ* in the remaining nations of the earth'. This race was the Nibelungs, 'to whom the earth belongs in name and for the happiness of every nation'. All this Ludwig had read and absorbed and by it he lived his life. For Ludwig, Wagner was as much a thinker and a prophet as he was a musician or an artist. Enabling the operas to be produced was simply a way of promoting the world view they contained. These teaching sessions were blissful for both men: whether they were the ideal preparation for a newly enthroned constitutional monarch may be questioned.

And while one love affair, however platonic, blossomed, so did another. When Ludwig was away, Wagner invited the Bülows to stay with him in his splendid house on the lake. Hans was ill, yet again, so only Cosima and their two daughters came; during this time, Cosima became pregnant with

Wagner's child. This consummation had been a long time coming. Not a year earlier, they had admitted their love to each other: 'We gazed speechless into each other's eyes; an intense longing for an avowal of the truth mastered us and led to a confession – which needed no words – of the boundless unhappiness which oppressed us.' Other people's unhappiness was soon to follow.

Now that he had breathing space, that he was no longer on the run from either creditors or governments, and that his artistic ambitions seemed capable of fulfilment, Wagner began to feel his usual restless energy surging up within him. In such a state, he always needed to unsettle the status quo. Since he felt that his recent good fortune was simply his just dessert, and had been arranged by destiny, he was not in the least circumspect about flaunting it. First he moved into a magnificent new house in town; not only did he furnish it to the very height of luxury, it was minutes away from the house once lived in by Lola Montez, the hated mistress of Ludwig's deposed grandfather, Ludwig I. The locals drew their conclusions: Wagner was quickly nicknamed Lola II, or Lolotte. He was oblivious; if he knew, he didn't care.

Next, confident in the unwavering support of his royal best friend, he applied himself with expansive energy to reforming the culture of opera in Munich. He started with the singers: current practitioners, he said, were nothing but 'a proletariat of the arts'. He needed a new breed of singer, an aristocracy of artists, and for that an opera academy like none other would be required; he set forth detailed and elaborate plans as to how it might be organised. Next he needed, he said, a new theatre capable of accommodating the titanic staging demands of *The Ring*; both the exquisite Cuvilliés theatre, one of the most beautiful in Europe, and the larger and brilliantly equipped National Theatre, were, he said, woefully inadequate. With each of these thrustful initiatives he instantly made himself a small army of enemies. Ludwig, besotted though he was, was no fool, and he saw that the proposed opera academy would annoy too many people with vested interests. He was not, however, at all averse to the idea of the new theatre. A site was found, and Wagner's friend Gottfried Semper, the architect of the old Dresden opera house, was commissioned to design it. He produced a model of a magnificent theatre, with a dramatic approach from the royal palace, through the city, across the river Isar and up a slight hill to a superbly commanding position in Steinhausen. Wagner and Semper worked together closely; the composer had a thorough grasp of architectural principles absorbed during the severe bout of erysipelas he had endured ten years earlier. The auditorium was to be austere and uncluttered, and feature a sunken orchestra pit, a radical notion of the importance of which Wagner had long been convinced. He drew up a schedule of performances: only *his* operas, naturally. Not only did he programme *Tannhäuser*, *Lohengrin* and the still unperformed *Tristan and Isolde*, he scheduled *The Ring of the Nibelung* and *The Mastersingers of Nuremberg* (both as yet incomplete) as well as *Parsifal* and *The Victors*, neither of which existed except as mere sketches. It is a staggering six-year plan. Perhaps the most extraordinary thing about it is that, with the exception of *The Victors*, he did it all, though not in Munich, and that each of the operas he planned proved to be a titanic masterpiece.

Ludwig was behind him all the way, and in one sense exceeded even Wagner's ambition, because he planned to rebuild the playhouse at the same time, creating a huge repertory of classics from all over the world and from all periods; he even proposed staging Ibsen's then wildly controversial plays. Together he and Wagner hatched a vision of Munich as a City of Art. For a while it seemed possible, though political opposition was fierce: Wagner was radical and expensive and, wholly confident of the king's support, comported himself as though he were omnipotent. But he had a formidable enemy in Ludwig's court: the Bavarian prime minister Baron Karl von der Pfordten had first encountered the composer in 1848 in Dresden as minister of education; he loathed Wagner, cordially detesting him for his part in the 1849 uprising. 'If the princes would only hold together as democrats do,' he had declared, 'Wagner's music would not be given anywhere.' Wagner was a marked man from the moment he arrived in Munich.

The Bülows, meanwhile, had moved there; at Wagner's urging Hans was appointed Court Pianist. Wagner conducted *The Flying Dutchman* at the Court Theatre, its first outing in Munich; it was a triumph. *Tristan and Isolde* was announced for the following year, with Bülow conducting. On the first day of rehearsals, 10 April 1865, the child Wagner had given Cosima was born; she was named Isolde, after the heroine of the opera in which, of course, a man betrays his best friend. The child's second name was Ludowika, after Ludwig. Bülow, who seems to have been unaware that Isolde was not his daughter, conducted the premiere of the opera superbly; the singers, carefully coached, acquitted themselves gloriously. The central characters were sung by the husband and wife team of Ludwig and Malwine Schnorr von Carolsfeld, and Tristan's faithful servant Kurwenal by Anton Mitterwurzer (the original Wolfram in *Tannhäuser*), all of them entirely to Wagner's satisfaction. The press, unsettled both by the plot and the unprecedented intensity and adventurousness of the music, was hostile. 'We think that the stage presentation of the poem *Tristan und Isolde* amounts to an act of indecency,' harrumphed the *Allgemeine musikalische Zeitung*. 'Wagner does not show us the life of heroes of Nordic sagas which would edify and strengthen the spirit of his German audiences. What he does present is the ruination of the life of heroes through sensuality.' Hanslick remarked that the prelude reminded him of 'the Italian painting of the martyr whose intestines are slowly being unwound from his body on a reel'. Such comments attempted to shut the barn door after the horse had bolted. The damage, if damage it was, had been done. Musicians everywhere were astounded at what Wagner had opened up with his harmonic audacity: the famous chord in the fourth bar of the Prelude which resolves itself into a dissonance – the famous *Tristan* chord – leads on to a series of unresolved cadences which do not find resolution until the very end of the opera. This is the apotheosis of suspension, both in the musical and the Schopenhauerian sense. And music would never be the same again.

Ludwig and Wagner were delirious. 'My Unique one! My Holy one!' wrote Ludwig, orgasmically, as if he were Isolde himself:

> How blissful!
> Perfect. So overcome with delight!

> To drown ... to sink – unconscious – highest pleasure –
>   Divine work!

> Eternally
> true to – beyond
> the grave.

But a black cloud descended: just six weeks after the first night the Tristan, Schnorr von Carolsfeld, a giant of a singer who had, despite delicate health, performed superbly, died – exhausted, it was darkly rumoured, by the impossible demands of the part; he was twenty-nine. 'Farewell Siegfried!' he cried, at the end, from his deathbed. 'Console my Richard!'

Ludwig knew very well how to console his Richard. Wagner went to stay with the king at the perfectly Wagnerian castle of

Hohenschwangau, in the centre of the old Swan district, its walls covered with murals depicting the German legends, notably Parzival and Lohengrin; it was here, surrounded by images of swans, that the young Ludwig had grown up. Here he and Wagner held lofty discourse into the small hours; at sunrise, oboists carefully placed across the castle turrets played themes from *Lohengrin*. Ludwig wrote to Cosima: 'Oh, he is godlike! Godlike! My mission is to live for him, to suffer for him, if that be necessary for his full salvation.' That was precisely Cosima's mission, as it happens, though Ludwig was blissfully ignorant of the now all-consuming relationship between them, a relationship that was already the subject of scandal in the coffee houses of Munich and even in the press; Wagner's personal extravagance and the prohibitive cost of staging his operas were the subject of further angry gossip. At this point, Wagner, with his total inability to gauge a situation except in his own terms, started enthusiastically meddling in Bavarian politics, writing 'anonymous' articles in the press, whose authorship was an open secret. Before long, Ludwig's exasperated prime minister delivered the king an ultimatum: he had to choose between the love of his people and his friendship with Richard Wagner. Ludwig was smart enough to know that, realistically speaking, he had no choice. That evening, while the composer was sitting in his splendid home by his magnificent fireside, an official came to inform him that the king had decreed that he must leave immediately. Dumbfounded, Wagner showed the official a passionate letter from the king signed: 'yourself unto death, until we cross to the next world, eternally, eternally, your truest Ludwig'. The official, unmoved by these sublime sentiments, was adamant: he must go. Two days later, Wagner was yet again on a train to Switzerland, with servant and dog. The fairy tale had been ruptured; he was an exile once more.

A very comfortable one, it has to be said. He soon settled in Lucerne, in a luxurious villa called Tribschen, with a superb view of the lake; it was all paid for, of course, by Ludwig, who, in his dejection at the turn of events, threatened to renounce the throne altogether. 'If it is the wish of the Dear One,' he wrote to Wagner, 'I will gladly renounce the throne and its barren splendour, come to him and never part from him.' Wagner swiftly dissuaded him: an ex-king was of no use to him. But for Ludwig being king had ceased to be fun: scheduled to open parliament, he chose instead to visit Wagner in Tribschen on his birthday. He stayed for two nights, after which, refreshed and restored, he went back to Munich, only then condescending to perform his official duties. The story slipped out; there was outrage. The press openly attacked Wagner, exposing his relationship with Cosima; Bülow caught wind of the accusations. After challenging the editor of one of the offending newspapers to a duel, he went to Switzerland to confront the guilty couple, who denied everything. Wagner got Ludwig to sign a letter he had drafted for him, denouncing the press's claims. That, too, would eventually blow up in Wagner's face, but for the time being, some sort of normality resumed.

For him, that is. In the non-fairy-tale world, a very real dragon was abroad, breathing fire: Prussia, having steadily built up its military might, was beginning to move in on the rest of the German-speaking world. In July 1866, Bavaria fought in the Austro-Prussian war on the Austrian side – an alliance of weakness that presented the Prussians with no challenge. 'A Bavarian,' remarked Bismarck, the Prussian chancellor, 'is someone halfway between an Austrian and a human being.' Ludwig was not, to put it mildly, of a military disposition, though he was rather keen on soldiers. Once, he spotted a sentry at the Residenz who looked tired, so he sent out a sofa for him. At first Ludwig wanted to have nothing to do with the war, and was reluctant to sign the mobilisation order, preferring to divert himself with firework displays; but Wagner persuaded him to be a king and lead his army, which he did, briefly. Even the soldiers were astonished by his youthful beauty, which momentarily rallied them; but the Bavarian army in its operetta uniforms (designed by Ludwig) had no hope against the streamlined forces that Prussia, with its universal conscription, its needle guns and its dedicated railways, could command. From now on Prussia's imperial ambition would dominate Bavarian public affairs; war was constantly on the agenda. Ludwig loathed it, and so, more surprisingly, did Wagner.

Wagner's domestic life had meanwhile undergone a transformation: Minna, worn out by illness and disappointment, but never having entirely given up on Wagner, had died in Dresden, at the age of fifty-seven. 'May the pitiful woman's tormented heart finally find rest!!' Wagner wrote to her doctor, with genuine feeling. He never got over the conviction that he had done her a disservice by marrying her, despite the fact that that she was, for a sizeable portion of the twenty years of their marriage, exactly what he needed – a provider of domestic comfort and companionship. 'Right from the beginning,' Minna had written fifteen years earlier, 'I did *everything* for *love of you*. My *independence* which I treasured so much, I gave up gladly, so that I really *could be yours alone*. As for your intellectual development, I am happy in the knowledge that *all* the beauty you created had come to life in the *home that I had made*.' And he knew it was true. She had kept him going. But now he had found someone very different who would guarantee the final triumph of his work; she was the person he now needed. 'Cosima must be with me. Always,' he wrote. 'Without her, nothing can be done. With her, I believe, I shall be able to work at my artistic productions until the end.'

She had come to stay in Tribschen, with her three daughters. Bülow joined them after a month, then they all left; four weeks later, Cosima came back without Bülow, but with the girls. In the midst of all this, Wagner, after a two-year gap, again picked up work on *The Mastersingers of Nuremberg*. In February, Cosima gave birth to Wagner's second daughter, whom they named Eva after the heroine of the new opera; six months later, he finally completed the score, which he presented to Ludwig on Christmas Day – Cosima's birthday, as it happens (or at least the day on which she celebrated it. She was born on 24th December, but both she and Wagner, bent on endowing everything in their lives with significance, always spoke of the 25th as her birthday). But this year, she was no longer with Wagner: she and the girls had gone back to Munich, to the Bülow family home. Wagner himself returned to Munich to supervise the first production of *The Mastersingers*, which Bülow conducted; Wagner stayed with the Bülows. Rehearsals were not without tension. Things between Wagner and Hans were predictably difficult, and Wagner's constant interventions in the musical rehearsals finally drove the orchestra to go on strike, led by the fiery horn player, Franz Strauss, whose four-year-old boy, Richard, would before very long become Wagner's operatic heir.

The Munich audience was enchanted by *The Mastersingers of Nuremberg* – and surprised, as the rest of the world has been ever since. It was so unexpected. *Tannhäuser*, *Lohengrin*, *The Ring*, *Tristan and Isolde*, *Parsifal* – even *The Flying Dutchman* – are all obviously the work of the same man, radically different from each other though they may be. They come from the same dark visionary imagination; they dwell in extremes. But *Mastersingers*, that cornucopious work, which is everything Wagner said an opera shouldn't be – brimming with tunes, arias, duets, ensembles, counterpoint, a huge chorus, spectacular public scenes, jokes, hijinks – recognisable human beings

– which wraps tendrils of voluptuous melody all around the work, casting a golden glow over the bourgeois communal life it celebrates – where was all that lurking inside the difficult, rebarbative, violently prejudiced, myth-forging, subconscious-probing, serially betraying, Schopenhauer-gorging, Feuerbach-chomping pessimist with his tragic view of life? In fact, *The Mastersingers of Nuremberg* is Wagner's most personal, most autobiographical work: he is both Sachs, the kindly but grizzled master, and Stolzing, the radical young pretender. It is also his most philosophically profound work, the one which embodies and exemplifies the idea to which he devoted his life, the idea of German art. But – with the exception of the punishment meted out to the reviled pedant, Beckmesser, on whom Wagner visits all his deep hatred of critics, punishing him as surely as Shakespeare punishes Malvolio in *Twelfth Night* – German art proves benevolent, embracing, capable of change and development, extending its blessing across the whole community. And at the end the community honours the great and wise artist at its centre:

'Hail Sachs! Hail Sachs!
Nuremberg's darling Sachs!'

It is true, of course, that if you probe the work, you will find melancholy, rage and an assertiveness about the supremacy of German art that is, on reflection, and in the light of events in the twentieth century, uncomfortable. The work has been probed in all these ways, not least at Bayreuth, but nobody was probing on that June night in 1868. There was a new element in the applause that night – affection. Wagner and the king risked disapproval by sitting together, side by side, in the royal box, in which, till then, only royalty and its descendants had ever sat; the aristocracy were even more deeply scandalised when Ludwig encouraged the composer to stand up at the end of each act to accept the generous applause, which he, Ludwig, led – this 'wonderful, unique' boy, still only twenty-two – whom Wagner loved as deeply and as tenderly as he had loved anyone.

Ludwig was more than ever dependent on his relationship with Wagner. In 1867, under huge ministerial pressure to produce an heir, he had become engaged to the Duchess Sophia Charlotte in Bavaria, an excellent dynastic match: her sister was the Empress of Austria. It was a mutual passion for Wagner that had brought them together: in his letters Ludwig addressed her as 'my dear Senta, Elisabeth, Isolde, Eva, Brunnhilde', which was quite something to live up to. It must have been a form of play-acting for both of them: Ludwig had told her, before their engagement, that he would never marry her because he would not live long, his life being linked to the continued existence of Wagner – 'the Friend' – who would, alas, inevitably perish before him. After that, Ludwig told Sophie Charlotte, his star would no longer shine, sundered from 'the remarkable, sweeping destiny of R Wagner'. He even addressed her in the letter in which (to the dismay of his subjects) he broke off the engagement as Elsa, the heroine of *Lohengrin*, signing himself Heinrich, the Fowler king from the same opera. None of this will have come as a surprise to Sophie Charlotte. Wagner, Ludwig had told her at the beginning of their relationship, was the God of his life.

Just a year after the triumphant first night of *The Mastersingers of Nuremberg*, the relationship between idol and idolater was in shreds. Ludwig, impatient to see *The Ring*, which, after all, he owned, started to plan a production at the charming Greek Revival-style National Theatre in Munich. Wagner tried to dissuade him: *The Ring* could only work in a custom-built theatre, he patiently explained, for the hundredth time, and it had to be seen in its entirety. But Siegfried, the wonderful, impulsive boy, defied Wotan, and in due course rehearsals for

Rheingold began in the face of Wagner's violent opposition. The young Austrian-Hungarian conductor, Hans Richter, Wagner's nominee and his representative during rehearsals, proved tiresome and was sacked. 'Get your hands off my score, sir,' Wagner growled at the cowering substitute conductor, 'or may the devil take you!' Even Ludwig's patience with Wagner ran out: 'in the end [this behaviour] will get out of control … it must be pulled up by the roots … *j'en ai assez*'. Fuming impotently, Wagner withdrew, boycotting the production, so the first instalment of the work over which Wagner had laboured for so many years had its world premiere – like *Lohengrin* – in the composer's absence. When *The Valkyrie* was produced the following year, he boycotted that, too. To stop Ludwig from getting his hands on *Siegfried*, he delayed putting the finishing touches to it, even though he had already started composing *The Twilight of the Gods*. That was how petty, how childish, it had become. The fairy tale was going to have a drastically unhappy ending, it seemed, after all. But now at least he knew there was nothing for it: if *The Ring* was to make its proper effect – if it was to do its revolutionary work – he would have to build the theatre of which he had so long dreamed himself. No one was going to do it for him.

At least he was not on his own any more. There had been more *va-et-vient* between Bülow's household and Wagner's, but in autumn of 1868, Cosima and the children settled in Tribschen for good; in 1870, Hans and Cosima finally divorced. 'You are determined to devote your life to a man much greater than myself,' Bülow wrote to her, 'and I must admit that your choice is right. My one consolation is: Cosima is happy now. I now must separate myself completely and utterly from you and from Richard Wagner, the two inspirations of my life.' Cosima confided in her diary: 'It seems to me cruel that I had to leave Hans. I feel it keenly that a divine decree willed it so, and I had no choice.'

A few months later, Cosima and Wagner married. She was thirty-three, he was fifty-nine. As he had said five years earlier: there was no question about it, she belonged to him. They made an odd couple to look at: she was Amazonianly tall, with severe, beaky features; he was uncommonly short, with a somewhat simian lope. But it was a perfect match. They were of one mind: his. She saw him as a Sublime Master, which helped him; Minna had always seen him as the needy, difficult, gifted boy she had first fallen in love with. Minna had tried to provide a nest for him; Cosima built him Valhalla. Intellectually and musically sophisticated, she was his helpmeet, and Wagner welcomed her input; sometimes he even changed things on her advice. Before long, she gave him a son and heir. She gave him, in fact, a life fit for a hero. And she was always at his side.

It was in 1869, after a gap of twelve years, having in the interim had a life-changing exposure to the work of Schopenhauer and written two massive and ground-breaking operas, that Wagner finally resumed his work on *Siegfried*. Ludwig was the first to know: 'The Shining Light came to see me – moved, plans to complete the Ring des Nibelungen,' he wrote in his diary. 'Joy Inconceivable.' Wagner's concept of music-drama, his political views, his understanding of the meaning of life, had all changed fundamentally. He made substantial amendments to the libretto: especially to *The Twilight of the Gods*. Now love – deep, transcendent self-obliviating physical love, in the Schopenhauerian sense – becomes the only reality. Power – all power – is not merely corrupting, it is an illusion. 'I shall try to tell you today of *Siegfried*,' he wrote to Ludwig before their falling-out:

It is with dread and with trepidation that I approach the composition of Act III. Here I am face to face with the central point of the cosmic drama. The end of the world is at hand, but it will be followed by re-birth, by regeneration. All this is sublime, terrible and mysterious. The music of the end came to me on my lonely mountain walks, in a storm: the jubilation of Siegfried and Brünnhilde, the proud pair united beyond life, beyond death.

As he finished the sketches for Act III of *Siegfried*, his son was born, and was inevitably given the young hero's name. Because of the deep estrangement between Ludwig and Wagner over Munich productions of *The Rhinegold* and *The Valkyrie*, he went no further with *Siegfried*, instead rapidly sketching out *The Twilight of the Gods* and dreaming of the theatre in which it would eventually be heard.

ELEVEN

Towards the Green Hill

At Tribschen the household consisted of Wagner, Cosima, Daniela and Blondine (Cosima's daughters from von Bülow), Isolde, Eva, and Siegfried, a governess, a housekeeper, a nanny, a manservant, two stable lads, a parlourmaid and a French cook, in addition to another Newfoundland dog, a terrier, two peacocks (Wotan and Erda), two golden pheasants, a cat, and an assortment of sheep and hens. In the house itself, Cosima created the environment in which Wagner could flourish, socially and creatively, which was a curious mixture of classical severity and intense voluptuousness. The latter he required for his work:

> If I am to do this, if I am once more to renounce reality – if I am to plunge once more into the woes of artistic fancy in order to find tranquillity in the world of imagination, my fancy must at least be helped. I cannot live like a dog; I cannot sleep on straw and drink bad liquor. My excitable, delicate, ardently craving and uncommonly soft and tender sensibility must be coaxed in some ways if my mind is to accomplish the horribly difficult task of creating a non-existent world.

Ernest Newman noted that in his last years Wagner could not work at all unless surrounded by soft lines and colours and perfumes. 'Such was the creator of the heroic, athletic, boy Siegfried,' wrote Ernest Newman, 'this poor little sickly, sensitive, self-indulgent neurotic who could hardly deny himself the smallest of his innocent little voluptuousnesses.' In the living room were tapestries, a Buddha, Chinese incense burners, cabinets with butterflies pinned to cards; in the study itself, heavy draperies, two book-lined walls, the Erard piano (made to look like an altar, with drawers and a table-top) and a portrait of Ludwig. This voluptuousness extended to Wagner's taste in garments, notably undergarments, which was widely discussed after the sensational appearance in 1877 of *Wagner's Letters to a Seamstress*, which revealed in extraordinary detail his requirements; initially, at least, it seems to have been a means of relieving the endless itch of erysipelas, but even after that was vanquished he insisted on having only silk close to his skin, and everything lined with satin, to keep him warm; unexpectedly, according to the seamstress in question, Berthe Goldwag, he was always cold. His outer garments, self-designed, were eccentric in the extreme: loose, flowing, somehow medieval while at the same time being raffishly bohemian; an unholy amalgam of the wardrobes of *The Mastersingers* and *La Bohème*, always capped by what might be described as his trademark beret, which he would take off and put back on a hundred times in the course of a conversation. Conversation with Wagner was a bit of a rollercoaster: the French poet Catulle Mendès described him as being in perpetual motion, striding about, putting his hat on, taking it off, talking, talking, talking: 'sublime images, puns, turns of phrase, an endless flood, always disjointed, never repeating himself, words that were proud or tender, violent or comic. And now, laughing till you thought he would split his sides, now growing tearfully tender, now rising to the heights of prophetic ecstasy.'

The unending flow took in tales of his political life in Dresden, his childhood dreams, his escapades, sitting in the back row of the stalls and seeing Weber conduct, Schröder-Devrient ('the tenderest and greatest memory of his whole existence'), and the death of Schnorr von Carolsfeld, who had created the role of Tristan: 'and as he spoke the word "Tristan", one felt a tremendous all-consuming sense of exaltation at the febrile eternity of the *Liebestod*, a state of frenetic nirvana! And all the while we sat there, dazed and bemused, laughing with him, weeping with him, sharing his feelings of joy, seeing his visions and submitting to the terror and charm of his imperious words like sun-flecked motes of dust at the tempest's mercy.'

Mendès's wife, the poet Judith Gautier, wrote that 'in the face of the Master, his beaming eyes, were blended the most beautiful shades of sapphire – that is what I saw, and I said to Mme Cosima, who thought quite as I did – "Now, at last, I comprehend that happiness of paradise, so extolled by believers, the seeing of the god face to face."' (Gautier had a brief affair with Wagner but Mme Cosima quickly nipped that in the bud.) Ludwig described him as 'the Shining Light', the 'Sun of Life', and much else besides of an equally elemental nature. This is the effect he had on those who were susceptible to him. Others found him simply alarming.

Edouard Schuré, esotericist and dramatist, was so overpowered by his experience of *Tristan* that he determined to make Wagner's acquaintance. He subsequently wrote a two-volume work on music-drama (*Richard Wagner: His Work and Ideas*), but later fell out with the composer as the cult around him grew. It was to Schuré that Wagner had confessed that his daemon was 'a frightful monster'. Schuré provides ample proof of it. 'To look at him,' wrote Schuré, 'was to see turn by turn in the same visage the front face of Faust and the profile of Mephistopheles … one stood dazzled before that exuberant and protean nature, ardent, personal, excessive in everything, yet marvellously equilibrated by the predominance of a devouring intellect.' Wagner had, it seemed, no inhibitions whatever, his qualities and defects on open display, to the delight of some and the deep repugnance of others. 'His gaiety flowed over in a joyous foam of facetious fantasies and extravagant pleasantries; but the least contradiction provoked him to incredible anger. Then he would leap like a tiger, roar like a stag. He paced the room like a caged lion, his voice became hoarse and the words came out like screams; his speech slashed about at random. He seemed at these times like some elemental force unchained, like a volcano in eruption. Everything in him was gigantic, excessive.' It is this very disinhibition that is at the root of his work: a willingness – indeed, a compulsion – to share what is deepest within him with the world at large.

If by any chance he did not find himself the centre of attention, he took swift remedial action. Robert von Hornstein (recipient of one of Wagner's most egregiously haughty begging letters, as we have seen) describes a pleasant gathering at Wagner's house which was suddenly interrupted by a blood-curdling scream. Electrified, the guests turned to see what the problem was, only to find the composer, sitting on a chair in the middle of the room, quite unperturbed. 'I've just been re-reading *The Golden Pot* by E. T. A. Hoffmann,' he remarked, pleasantly. 'I'll read it to you.' It is not a short story. When he eventually came to an end, Otto Wesendonck, who was present, mildly commented that he had no time for that sort of romanticism, at which Wagner fell into a ranting tirade that had still not subsided by the time the traumatised guests crept away. Often he would sing for his guests. The composer-journalist Ferdinand Praeger compared his singing to the barking of a Newfoundland dog; it was nonetheless strangely compelling, said Praeger, and invariably accompanied by large inhalations of snuff. On one occasion he ran out of it, refusing to continue until more was found. 'No snuff,' he said, 'no singing.' A midnight search for the precious substance began, and when some was found, he started up again.

He seems to have delighted in presenting different faces to different people. To the intense young philology teacher, Friedrich Nietzsche, whom he met on a visit to Leipzig during a brief escape from the endless emotional turmoil at Tribschen, he spoke in the measured tones of a great philosopher. Nietzsche, shy and almost monosyllabic in his presence, instantly fell under the spell of the Master. After he took up an appointment as the youngest professor at the University of Basel, he became a regular visitor of the Wagners in nearby Lucerne. 'Tribschen,' Nietzsche wrote to his intimate friend, Rohde, 'has become a second home for me. In recent weeks I have been there four times in rapid succession, and a letter passes between us at least once a week. My dearest friend, what I learn and see there is indescribable. Schopenhauer and Goethe, Aeschylus and Pindar are still alive, believe me.' It swiftly became the central relationship of Nietzsche's life, emotionally and intellectually, even after – particularly after – he had turned against Wagner; almost his last words, as he lay dying of the ravages of what appears to have been a virulent form of syphilis, were of Cosima. In fact, it was a three-way relationship, what psychoanalysts refer to as a double cathexis, in which Nietzsche made a huge emotional investment in both Wagners. With Cosima the relationship was semi-erotic; with Wagner himself it was a relationship of service, verging on servility, in which Nietzsche was tasked with writing articles and delivering speeches which expressed the official view, which was often explicitly anti-Semitic. Nietzsche kow-towed, though he had no previous record of anti-Semitism, and later abhorred it. He was also given small domestic errands to perform – getting Wagner's books rebound, for example, or tracking down a portrait of Adolf Wagner, Wagner's beloved antiquarian uncle – a surprising use of his time for a doctor of philosophy and professor of philology.

By far the most significant outcome of Nietzsche's devotion to Wagner was his first book, *The Birth of Tragedy from the Spirit of Music*, in which he first adumbrates his famous opposition between Apollonian and Dionysiac modes, introducing Socrates as anti-hero, the enemy of tragedy, forever rationalising life, striving for optimism (as a result of which the drama takes what he calls 'the death-leap into bourgeois theatre'). Anyone familiar with Wagner's table-talk would have concluded that Nietzsche had been listening to it keenly; in *his* first book, *Art and Revolution*, Wagner had made much of the opposition between Dionysus and Apollo. Seeing that *The Birth of Tragedy* admirably promoted the Master's view of life and art – notably the supremacy of the latter over the former – Wagner and Cosima, on the whole, approved of the book. From Nietzsche's point of view, Wagner perfectly embodied the quest for the ecstatic with which the philosopher scornfully contrasted the Socratic, rational approach that Wagner expressly renounced. 'What makes you see or wish to see a wise man in me?' he had written to Judith Gautier during their brief liaison: 'How can I be a wise man, I who am myself only when in a state of raving frenzy?'

Unlike Wagner, Nietzsche's entire experience of ecstasy seems to have been confined to art, and Wagner's music purveyed it in its most concentrated form. Of *Tristan* he said: 'I am still looking for a work with as dangerous a fascination, with as terrible and as sweet an affinity. I simply cannot bring myself to remain critically aloof from this music; every nerve in me a-twitch, and it has been a long time since I had such a lasting sense of ecstasy.' Apart from the incident in which, presumably, he had contracted syphilis (although there is a suggestion that he may have inherited it from his clergyman father), Nietzsche seems never to have known a consummated love, though his male friendships were of exceptional intensity. 'Everything my friend Rohde feels,' he told Wagner and

Cosima, 'I feel also, thus doubling my pleasure.' Cosima replied that – 'as our liege has told us' – Wagner entirely approved of such relationships; after all, he said, 'the adoration of women is a completely new phenomenon which radically divides us from the ancient world'. Nietzsche felt approved of, endorsed, empowered by both Cosima and Richard. He became absorbed into the household: he was in Tribschen during the agonising birth of Siegfried, and he was among the select few to be present at the famous first performance of the *Tribschen Idyll with Fidi's birdsong and the orange sunrise, as symphonic birthday greeting* (later known as the *Siegfried Idyll*) with which thirteen musicians, ranged all the way up the staircase, awoke Cosima on Christmas Day 1870, her thirty-third birthday. That night they performed a dramatisation of Wagner's favourite E. T. A. Hoffmann story *The Golden Pot* in which, with none too subtle symbolism, Wagner took the leading part of the magician Archivarius Lindhorst, while Nietzsche – Professor Nietzsche – played the idiot factotum who copies the master's manuscripts and trips over apple baskets. Wagner saw a great deal of potential in Nietzsche – he could, for example, be very useful in bringing up the boy-hero to whom Cosima had so recently given birth; he even laid plans for the child to travel to whatever academic seat Nietzsche might occupy. As it happens, Nietzsche never occupied another university chair: *The Birth of Tragedy*, a philosophical fantasia devoid of scholarship and savagely criticised by his colleagues, had destroyed his academic future, though he continued to teach at Basel for another decade. This was neither here nor there from Wagner's point of view; as far as he was concerned he had acquired an assistant and occasional mouthpiece, who would come in very handy during the great task Wagner was about to take up: the creation of the theatre of the future.

Cosima and Wagner had already embarked on the Great Task. They had been invited by the town council of the small

Bavarian town of Bayreuth to look at the beautiful baroque Markgräfliches Opernhaus – the Margravial Opera House – but despite the uncommon size of its stage it was clearly no more suitable for *The Ring* than the Court Theatre in Munich; Wagner dismissed it out of hand. Instead, he decided he would build a new theatre on a little hill he had spotted just beyond the town centre. The town council, delighted and honoured, gave him the land. At the same, Wagner bought a nearby plot on which to build a house for himself, to which he gave the Wagnerian-Schopenhauerian name of *Wahnfried*: 'rest from illusion'. Ludwig, now slowly warming to Wagner again, gave him 25,000 thalers to build it. But rest was the last thing Wagner got. Money had to be raised, large amounts of it. He conducted a concert in Berlin, attended by the newly created Kaiser, Wilhelm I; unsolicited, he wrote a wildly bombastic *Kaisermarsch* for the inauguration of the newfangled German Reichstag and the newfangled German monarchy. It was rejected. He met the chancellor, Bismarck, architect of the new German Empire, and tried to convince him to invest, on behalf of the new German nation, in the great German work of art he was creating; but Bismarck demurred. Wagner roamed Europe, and beyond, conducting concerts and addressing the faithful, all the while toiling over the still incomplete scores of *Siegfried* and *The Twilight of the Gods*; his health was not good. At one point, not for the first or the last time, he toyed with moving to America, where there were enthusiastic Wagner societies comprised largely of German expatriates, eager to welcome him. Instead he threw his energy into encouraging the formation of Wagner societies around the world.

Finally, on his fifty-ninth birthday, 22 May 1872, the foundation stone for the Festspielhaus was laid, in pouring rain; the ceremony then transferred to the opera house, where, incongruously surrounded by the gilt exuberance of its great baroque interior, the apostle of the work of art of the future spoke. He was deeply moved, saying how honoured he was, honoured as no other artist in history had been, which was true enough, though he had in fact bestowed the honour on himself. The theatre they were now starting to build, he said, was a temporary one, a mere makeshift: that, he tartly explained, was because the German parliament had refused to pay for it, and because of the deplorable condition of German art at present. Nonetheless, he said, in the proportions of the interior and in its seating arrangements, 'you will find the expression of an idea which, once grasped, will transform your expectations into something quite different from anything you have ever before experienced in visiting a theatre. If this effect is fully achieved,' he went on, 'the mysterious entry of the music will prepare you for the unveiling and display of scenic pictures which, by appearing to emanate from an idealistic dream world, should demonstrate to you the complete reality of the stimulating powers of a noble art.'

When he spoke of the 'mysterious entry of the music', he was, of course, referring to the famous invisible orchestra, hidden away under the stage, a long-held idea of his, originally inspired by the opera house in Riga, which was intended not simply to enhance the balance with the singers' voices, but to eliminate anything which came between the audience and the story. The purpose of theatre, he insisted, was not to engage with the analytical mind, but with the subconscious; the dream-like state he described offered access to deep, buried, maybe inchoate, emotions. This, he says, is the source of its power and profundity, and this is why theatre is central to society: it binds us together at the deepest level. Wagner used the speech to nail his theatrical colours to the mast. The form of theatre that he was seeking to create, that the Festspielhaus existed to realise, is the polar opposite of the sort of theatre – Brecht's for example, or George Bernard

Shaw's – which strives to engage the conscious mind, to stimulate consciousness, in fact, in the political as well as the mental sense. In Brecht's theatre, every member of the audience is a critic. In Wagner's the artist/priest/conjuror is in total command; your job as a member of the audience is to submit. So whatever the political agenda of *The Ring* might have been – and as we have seen, that had changed over the years of composition – the theatrical means Wagner employed could never have bred an assessing, an analytical, attitude in the audience. His aim was spiritual and visceral; his was an anti-Socratic theatre, neither rational nor optimistic. Wotan is the loser in *The Ring* because 'he resembles *us* to a tee; he is the sum total of present-day intelligence, whereas Siegfried is the man of the future whom we desire and long for but who cannot be made by us, since he must create himself on the basis of *our own annihilation*'.

Wagner ended his speech at the Margravial Theatre with a ringing assertion of the standards he intended to maintain: 'Here nothing must be permitted to speak in mere provisional, sketchy forms; in scenery and in acting you will be offered the best that the artistic skills of our times can achieve.' In response to this promise, the chorus – specially assembled, like the orchestra – gave hearty vent to *Wacht auf!*, the great cry with which Sachs is greeted at the end of *The Mastersingers of Nuremberg*:

> Wake up! dawn is drawing near;
> I hear a blissful nightingale
> singing in the green grove,
> its voice rings through hill and valley;
> night is sinking in the west,
> the day arises in the east,
> the ardent red glow of morning
> approaches through the gloomy clouds.

Then, as a ringing assertion of what German art could be, and should be, he conducted Beethoven's Choral Symphony. 'Everything that had happened up to now,' wrote Nietzsche, in a pamphlet to accompany the occasion, 'was a preparation for this moment.'

It was four years before the theatre was ready to open. Wagner spent all of 1873 touring Germany, partly to enlist singers and players, mostly to raise money by conducting concerts and giving electrifying fundraising readings of the libretto of *The Twilight of the Gods*. But however much he raised it was never enough, and two years after the laying of the foundation stone, and despite Nietzsche's exhortation to the public 'to support to the fullest extent possible this great artistic act of the German genius', building ground to a halt. For the second time in his life, Wagner was saved by Ludwig, still, despite their estrangement, the perfect Wagnerite. The king bailed him out again with an enormous loan. 'No, no, and again *no*!' he wrote to Wagner, 'It should not end thus! Help must be given! Our plan dare not fail. Parzival knows his mission, and will offer whatever lies in his powers.' Building resumed. Through all of this, Wagner continued toiling over the vast score; by 1874, a quarter of a century after the first sketch had been made, *The Twilight of the Gods* was finally complete. There were more and more fundraising concerts, in extended tours across Europe: he was becoming an international superstar. 'When he conducts he is almost beside himself with excitement,' wrote the American pianist Amy Fay. 'That is one reason why he is great as a conductor, for the orchestra catches his frenzy, and each man plays under a sudden inspiration. He really seems to be improvising on his orchestra.' In early 1876, he staged both *Lohengrin* and *Tannhäuser* in Vienna, with Richter conducting; the following year, the city finally saw *Tristan and Isolde*. The proceeds of these productions were, like everything else, gobbled up into the all-consuming Festspielhaus fund.

Meanwhile, a full two years before the first public performances, preliminary rehearsals began under Richter. Rehearsals continued throughout 1875. 'It is perhaps for the first time in your artistic careers, that you are called to dedicate your powers to the realisation of such a unique artistic objective,' Wagner wrote to the singers he invited to be part of the first festival, detailing the extensive work that would be required; care would be taken, he said, not to overwork and fatigue any of the artists. 'We wish to demonstrate to German audiences what German artists can achieve in their own native art. I now expect your declaration to the effect that you pledge your willingness to help realise a unique artistic ideal.' The orchestra, selected and led by the great violinist August Wilhelmj, was recruited from all over Germany, as were the singers and the dancers and the acrobats who played Hunding's horde and operated the dragon. At the end of the 1875 rehearsals, Wagner threw a party at the Haus Wahnfried for no less than 140 artists.

The scale of what they were undertaking is mind-boggling: merely opening a new theatre, with all its operational teething problems, is quite challenging enough, but to do so with not one but four new operas, on four consecutive nights – each one with staging nightmares on every page – dragons breathing fire, horses flying through the air, descents into the underworld, a rainbow bridge, roofs flying off huts, funeral pyres and stage-engulfing floods – with a huge cast and an army of stage technicians, to say nothing of the musical demands of an unknown, immensely long and very complex score – verges on the insane. But there was a mad idealism in the air. No one was paid – 'anyone who does not come out of esteem and commitment,' Wagner declared, 'I shall leave where he is' – but they eagerly flocked from all over Germany, the best designers, singers, players in the land, while the entire musical world held its breath. *The Ring of the Nibelung* had been a long time coming.

The theatre, the largest half-timbered building erected up to that point, was ready on time, but only just. A month before rehearsals began, Wagner had been trying to play off the Prussian and Bavarian governments against each other in the hope of squeezing some money out of them, but failed. At last, humiliatingly, he begged Ludwig personally for a small further bridging loan, which that saintly monarch unhesitatingly extended to him. Final rehearsals could begin, two months of what Wagner called 'further study' of the cycle, with orchestra, scenery and costumes – an unparalleled luxury. Months, even years, of preparation had preceded the actual staging. Vast numbers of costumes, huge tracts of set, great hanging backcloths and a plethora of special effects had been designed and sent for construction. The latter were particularly troublesome: rainbows, dragons, magic fire, flying Rhinemaidens, collapsing palaces. They were farmed out to workshops all over Europe: the dragon, for example, was built by the pantomime specialist Richard Keene, of Milton Street, Wandsworth, in south London: it was deemed a great success, despite the non-arrival of its neck, which had been sent not to Bayreuth but to Beirut. Richter struggled with the singers, some of whom were grievously stretched by their roles, as were the orchestra, all 115 of them. Wagner advised, inspired and terrorised, directing, occasionally conducting, attending to every detail, no matter how small, despite having, throughout the rehearsal period, a raging abscess, to abate which his head was permanently wrapped in a bandage and cotton wool.

He was always more than willing to stop and put to rights anyone who was unclear about anything. At the first rehearsal of *The Valkyrie*, Wagner described to the struggling Sieglinde the precise gesture with which she should pass from frozen despair to startled joy and enraptured exultation, and when he demonstrated it, he made everyone cry. 'What an inspiring director he was!' wrote the impresario Angelo Neumann. 'How well he understood the art of spurring on his men, getting the best work out of each one, of making every gesture, each expression tell! These rehearsals convinced me that he was not only the greatest dramatist of all time, but also the greatest of directors, and a marvellous actor as well.' Wagner's unflagging energy was indispensable once the whole great leviathan was finally assembled: the technical rehearsals were every backstage nightmare rolled into one – or rather into four. Half the set was unfinished; the dragon (minus neck) arrived from Keene's workshops in London at the very last minute; singers were constantly losing their voices or their nerve; one of the orchestral violinists dropped dead; the Sieglinde, despite Wagner's personal input, was a catastrophe, and temperamental with it; the all-important technical manager, Herr Brandt, who co-ordinated the whole giant event, walked out when he discovered that he was described on the programme as a 'machinist'; the costumes for *The Twilight of the Gods* made the singers look like Red Indian chieftains; the Rhinemaidens were terrified of the flying devices they had to harness themselves to; they were rapidly running out of money, prompting Cosima to try to get her inheritance money from Paris to throw into the kitty; Brünnhilde's horse was too frisky, so had to be led off before she sang; the brilliant but overworked rehearsal pianist Joseph Rubinstein – 'who once more,' remarked Cosima, pleasantly, 'displayed all the dismal characteristics of his race' – was dismissed, again, and reinstated, again.

To everyone's amazement the magic fire actually worked.

Finally, ready or not, the first outing of the biggest single piece of theatre in the history of Western culture approached. One notable member of the audience jumped the queue. Ludwig of Bavaria came to the dress rehearsals to avoid having to fraternise with his fellow royals. 'They bore me to death,' he said. 'If they molest me, call the police.' Outwitting his adoring subjects, many of whom were milling around the streets of Bayreuth in anticipation of the great event, he got off the train a couple of stops up the line, where he was greeted by Wagner alone, and escorted in a closed carriage to the theatre and slipped into his box. He was utterly overwhelmed by what he saw. 'You are a god-man,' he wrote to Wagner afterwards, 'the true artist by God's grace who brought the sacred fire down from heaven to earth, to purify, to sanctify and to redeem! The god-man who truly cannot fail and cannot err!' Not words anyone ever addressed to Verdi – or indeed to Mozart or to Beethoven. But none of them had ever attempted what Wagner had at last achieved. The day before the first public performance of *The Rhinegold*, by which time Ludwig had disappeared, Wagner greeted the new Kaiser along with sundry grand dukes and duchesses. 'Well,' said Wilhelm to Wagner, 'you've finally done it.' Wagner somehow managed to refrain from answering: 'Yes, and with no help from you.'

Just before the curtain rose, Wagner pinned up a message for the cast, eminently practical: '*Clarity!* The big notes will take care of themselves; the small notes and the text are the main thing. Never address the audience but only one another; in monologues, always look up or down, never straight ahead. *Last request!* Be faithful to me, dear Friends.' Another went up in the orchestra pit: 'No prelude playing! Piano pianissimo – then all will be well.' Which admonition, as Frederic Spotts notes, remained there for nearly a hundred years.

At long last – at 6.30 p.m., on 12 August 1876, four years after the foundation stone of the theatre had been laid – the great unending triad of E-flat major which in a feverish half-awake state Wagner had heard with his inner ear in a seedy Italian hotel room twenty-three years earlier, finally seeped into the listeners' consciousness and *The Ring of the Nibelung* began its long journey in circumstances that, as Wagner had correctly predicted, no one had ever before experienced in a theatre: in the great austere amphitheatre, with its severely undecorated walls, the lights dimmed to invisibility and the orchestra nowhere to be seen, the Rhinemaidens swam into view from beyond the receding proscenium arches, emerging from endless black space, apparently underwater, singing their siren song. As Wagner said they would, they seemed to emerge from within a dream.

From that breathtaking moment on, pretty well everything that could go wrong did go wrong, most devastatingly when just before the first scene change the stagehands raised the backcloth too soon, revealing the back wall of the theatre, with the crew standing around in shirt sleeves and singers waiting to go on, suddenly caught like rabbits in the headlights. Wagner was consumed with rage, hurling down bitter imprecations on everyone's heads. Though the audience roared and roared for him at the end of the performance, he refused to come out, storming off into the night. He cheered up only when, a little later, he chanced upon Dom Pedro II, the Emperor of Brazil, who, unannounced and unattended, was staying at a local hotel, to which Wagner now escorted him. Dom Pedro was asked to sign the hotel register; under 'Occupation' he wrote 'Emperor', which amused Wagner inordinately. As he had told Judith Gautier, in the letter in which he had confessed to her that he was 'the maddest person imaginable', he had a vivid sense of humour 'which again and again helps me over abysses that the wisest man does not even see'.

Each of the three subsequent nights had their successes and their failures, but the cumulative effect was overwhelming, musically, dramatically and theatrically. In every area, Wagner had revolutionised the art. Even sceptics like Tchaikovsky had finally to acknowledge the grandeur of the enterprise: 'I think that everyone who believes in the civilising effect of art will agree that the Bayreuth Festival is a stupendous achievement … one thing that we can be sure of: that out children and their children will still be talking of Bayreuth.' Tchaikovsky was mildly cynical about Wagner, but even hostile witnesses were forced to admire what he had done. 'Whether or not the work meets all the expectations of the Bayreuth pilgrims,' wrote Eduard Hanslick, Wagner's most relentless critic, 'there is one thing in which all will be of one mind: in admiration of the extraordinary energy and capacity for work and agitation of the man who, on his own, conceived this phenomenon and carried it through to its conclusion.' This was magnanimous, since it was widely believed (by Hanslick, for one) that Wagner had based the character of the pernickety killjoy Beckmesser in *The Mastersingers of Nuremberg* on him. Grieg said that *The Ring* was 'the creation of a true giant in the history of art comparable in innovation only to Michelangelo'. Ludwig of Bavaria, now that the danger of bumping into another king or an emperor had receded, came back for more, attending the third and final cycle. At the end of *The Twilight of the Gods*, as the waters of the Rhine flooded the stage and the Rhinemaidens recovered their gold and love reigned triumphant, the king stood up in the royal box – specially installed for him – to applaud. Then Wagner took to the stage to acknowledge the ovation. Stilling the audience, he said: 'The Festival was embarked on in the German spirit and completed for the glory of the King of Bavaria, who has been not only a benefactor and a protector to me, but a co-creator of my work.' Which was handsome indeed. The applause went on and on.

Wagner was unmoved. The day after this last performance, Cosima noted in her diary: 'R is very sad, says he wishes he could die.' The effect over the four evenings had been stupendous: a wonder of the world. But it fell so far short in so many ways of what he had willed. The physical production, with designs by the Viennese landscape painter Josef Hoffmann, had been too literal – 'an archaeologist's fantasy', thought Cosima; 'fantasy in chains', Nietzsche called it. Everything, Wagner said, should have been simpler, more primitive. As it was, it was just *pretend*. The singers failed to penetrate to the heart of their characters; Richter's tempi were wayward. Next year, Wagner told Cosima, they would 'do it all differently'. But there was no next year, or the year after. The financial deficit was vast; they had not managed to shift all the seats, and it would be many years before they did on a regular basis. Wagner told his loyal supporters at Bayreuth that the next festival would not be until 1880, after which all his operas would be performed over three years, culminating in *Parsifal*, the work he was now actively engaged on. In fact, the next festival was in 1882, and it consisted of just that one work, which Wagner now brought forth with agonising difficulty and in intense physical pain, all the while trying to raise money.

Meanwhile the work that Bayreuth had been built to accommodate, the Art-work of the Future for which the Theatre of the Future had been conceived and constructed, and which Wagner had never intended to be played anywhere else, was released by Wagner into general circulation. Before long, there were stagings of *The Ring of the Nibelung* in Berlin and in Vienna; the impresario Neumann (a Jew) fearlessly took a touring version of the tetralogy, based on the Bayreuth production, to opera houses across Europe, including Paris and London, for which Wagner was deeply grateful: 'Neumann sees it as his calling in life to ensure that I am recognised throughout the world.' The work entered the mainstream. Wagner lost control of it, unable to guarantee for it, as he had so fervently hoped, a mentally and spiritually receptive audience for whom the performance would have been a sacred event. It had become part of the operatic marketplace, a commodity to be bought by the rich for money. Dreams of that theatre in the meadow, with its non-paying audiences, finally died. 'After a year's preparation,' he had said, ten years earlier, when staging *The Ring* had seemed like an impossible dream, 'I shall over four days present my complete work: with it I shall reveal to the people of the revolution the meaning of this revolution in its noblest sense ... wild as this plan is, it is the only one on which I can stake my life, my work and my endeavour.' By the time the Bayreuth theatre was built, the people of the revolution had been replaced by the crowned heads of Europe and the entire musical establishment.

Another casualty of that first season was Wagner's relationship with Nietzsche. In fact, Nietzsche, though he had tickets for the First Night, never crossed the threshold of the Festival Theatre. Repelled by the audience, he fled. 'The mistake was to go to Bayreuth with an ideal, so the result was bitter disappointment,' he wrote in his diary. 'All Europe's lazy rich vagabonds were there, together with that miserable pack of patrons and patronesses, all bored to death and totally uninterested in music. Wagner's ideal? The rabble didn't want to know.' There had been rumblings of rebellion from Nietzsche in the face of the evident lack of respect extended to him by the Wagners. His mutiny began in somewhat veiled form in 'Richard Wagner in Bayreuth', one of a series of essays called *Untimely Meditations*. The essay is described as a *Festschrift*, but its tone of celebration is undercut by a series of observations about Wagner which are at the very least equivocal and in some cases overtly hostile. The tone is essentially passive-aggressive, and can scarcely have been designed to please its subject: 'In fact, Wagner is not a composer at all,' writes Nietzsche, advancing a perception that he would elaborate over and over again in book after book, 'but an instinctive theatrical who, dissatisfied with the easy pickings that lay readily to hand, has forced his way into the other arts.' His characterisation of Wagner the man pulled no punches, either: 'deep down', he writes, 'there surges through Wagner a mighty will with a boundless, ruthless craving for power, working its way along paths, through caves and ravines, ever upwards towards the light, with the brutality of a horned Minotaur'. Wagner wrote to Nietzsche to congratulate him on the book; one can only assume that he had not yet read it. Not long after its appearance, Wagner wrote to Nietzsche's doctor to tell him that he believed Nietzsche to be seriously unstable mentally, and that this was doubtless due to excessive masturbation. Nietzsche was forgivably enraged both by the suggestion and by Wagner's having written to his doctor. The personal relationship between the two men was virtually at an end, but the image of Wagner as the mythic man-bull, at the centre of a terrifying labyrinth, preyed on Nietzsche's increasingly disturbed mind; by extension, he identified Cosima as Ariadne, guardian of the labyrinth. But Ariadne was also the lover of Dionysus, the destructive-creative, male-female, god of fertility, of ritual madness, of wine and of theatre – Wagner in yet another form. And so down the labyrinth of his own mind he chased these people who had so comprehensively penetrated his inner life. Wagner is never far from the surface of Nietzsche's books, and often he is their explicit subject, *The Case of Wagner* and *Nietzsche contra Wagner* among them. This was vexing to Wagner, but scarcely impinged on his 'mighty will'; as Bryan Magee has pointed out, it is perfectly possible to write about Wagner without mentioning Nietzsche, but impossible to write of Nietzsche without mentioning Wagner. It was a possession, which never let up till the day Nietzsche died.

TWELVE

The Long Day's Task is Done

Wagner reflected bleakly on the first season. Just as in *The Ring*, gold had poisoned everything. If the festival was to continue – and however corrupted it had been, however far from what he had imagined, he still held faith with the idea – he needed a great deal more money. He knew now that there were no more hidden patrons, no more mad kings with limitless funds waiting in the wings. He must raise the cash himself. He went back to London to conduct eight concerts at the Royal Albert Hall, under somewhat bizarre circumstances. His faltering health prevented him from conducting an entire concert, so after he had conducted an overture or an orchestral interlude, he would go and sit in an armchair at the side of the stage and listen, somewhat abstractedly, according to reports, while Richter conducted the rest of the programme. His old admirer, Queen Victoria, twenty-two years after their last meeting, with Prince Albert now long dead, invited him to Windsor Castle, where he conducted a whole concert for her. He went to a performance of *Tannhäuser* at Covent Garden of such ineptitude – it was in Italian, apart from anything else – that Wagner fled with some of his friends and holed up in a German restaurant in the Strand, where, over a chop and a pint of Bass's ale, he regaled them with Jewish folk tales, replete with authentic accents. As on his previous money-making visit to the city, he came away with much less cash than he had expected.

The Flying Dutchman opened in New York, to enormous acclaim, and Wagner again contemplated emigrating to the United States, the only place on the whole map, he told

Cosima 'again and again', on which he could look with any pleasure: 'What the Greeks were among the peoples of this earth, this continent is among its countries.' He actively tried to frame a deal whereby his American fans would raise a million dollars, 'half of which would buy me a suitable residence in a part of the States with a decent climate, while the other half would be deposited with a state bank, a capital investment, with an annual yield of five per cent'. In return, his investors would get the proceeds from *Parsifal*, which he was then writing, and any other work he might write. 'Thus would America have bought me from Europe for all time,' he said. The idea of buying a share in Wagner is a beguiling one, but it came to nothing. He had by now, after years of contemplation and distillation of myths and wide-ranging ritual imagery, finished the libretto for *Parsifal*, which in time-honoured fashion he now read to his friends. Weakened though he was – creating Bayreuth had taken a terrible toll of him – he cast his usual spell. 'The great actor-poet at his best,' said an English admirer. 'An improvisation perfectly balanced – every part stood forth as that of an individual – voice, enunciation, moderation, exquisite – especially Act II, the flower maidens and Amfortas. One heard the words, and one heard the latent music. Bayreuth in miniature.'

Bayreuth, of course, was conceived for *The Ring*; but *Parsifal* was conceived for Bayreuth. Next time they would do it all differently, he had said, and they did. No more spectaculars. The physical action was limited; atmosphere was paramount, inner life made manifest, the past permeating everything. The seeds of the libretto, which had lain dormant within him since that fertile summer of 1841 when the German legends started to take root in his subconscious, now flowered into a kind of luxuriant sick beauty. Wagner's libretto – poem – was a synthesis of legends and characters from different sources and diverse cultures, fused together by a sense of the desperation of the human condition and an excruciating longing for transcendence. The revivifying power of the Grail; the stuttering progress of the Holy Fool – Parsifal himself – towards enlightenment; the devastating illness of the wounded king, Amfortas; the impotent destructiveness of the castrated magician Klingsor; the paralysing self-loathing of Kundry, the sexually ravenous woman who saw Christ and was condemned never to die – all these archetypal images of suffering, bewildered mankind woven into a symphonic tissue of unearthly translucence.

He was now in constantly poor health; work on *Parsifal* proceeded slowly, informed by the pain he was never without: uncannily and disturbingly drawing forth from his orchestra the music of suffering, pain clothed in sound. He cancelled the announced 1880 festival, spending most of that year in Italy, with Cosima and the children, returning to Munich to attend performances of *The Flying Dutchman, Tristan and Isolde* and *Lohengrin* in the Court Theatre; he continued to be ill, and *Parsifal* proceeded, bar by bar, with agonising slowness. From November 1881 to April of the following year, the family, escaping the bleak Bayreuth climate, which Wagner had always detested, wintered in Italy: the work took shape under the inspiration of its light, its air, its churches, its gardens. In Ravello, on the Amalfi coast, he found Klingsor's magic garden; in Siena's cathedral he found the prototype for the Temple of the Grail. The painter and poet Paul Joukowsky was engaged to design the opera, in collaboration with Max Brückner, and he and his boyfriend travelled round with the Wagners, faithfully reproducing in the designs what they had seen. *Parsifal* was finally completed in Sicily, in the city of Palermo, after which they moved on to Acireale in Catania, and then on to Venice – always Venice.

Intensive preparations had begun the year before for the second festival; the Wagners returned to Bayreuth in May of

1882 for rehearsals for *Parsifal*, which, to fierce opposition from Wagner, was to be conducted by Ludwig's chief conductor, Hermann Levi, the son of a rabbi; since Ludwig had provided the court orchestra and chorus free of charge for the festival, Wagner had no option but to accept him, at which Ludwig wrote to him, delighted, he said, that Wagner made 'no distinction between Christian and Jew', which suggests an unsuspected capacity for irony in the king's temperament. 'There is nothing so nauseous, so unedifying, as disputes of this sort,' Ludwig continued, firmly. 'At bottom, all men are brothers, whatever their confessional differences.' In his reply to this letter, Wagner told Ludwig that the king's sympathetic view of Jews was due to the fact that he rarely met any: for him they were simply a concept, 'whereas for us, they are an empirical fact'. The Jewish race, he continued, was 'the born enemy of pure humanity and everything noble about it … there is no doubt that we Germans especially will be destroyed by them, and I may well be the last German who, as an artist, has known how to hold his ground in the face of a Judaism which is now all powerful …'. He consoled himself by trying, unsuccessfully, to convert Levi to Christianity.

The conductor seems to have taken it all in good part. Wagner reposed absolute trust in him musically and Levi adored Wagner, insisting in a letter to his father, the Rabbi, that the composer was, essentially, a good man; indeed, he stayed in Wagner's apartment on more than one occasion as a house guest. Rubinstein, the rehearsal pianist, was equally devoted to him, despite Wagner's insane racial tirades. On one occasion, the composer stood up and warmly thanked Rubinstein for his work, then said: 'If we never got closer as human beings, the fault is not mine but yours. You belong to a foreign race with which we have no sympathy.' From there his speech of thanks developed into a rant which embarrassed everyone, including himself. Never far from the surface of the towering visionary genius lurked the hooligan. At one point during rehearsals, Wagner pleasantly remarked that it would be no bad thing if a few stout local lads were to give Herr Hanslick – his critical nemesis – a sound thrashing next time he came to Bayreuth. That there should be a latent streak of violence in the composer of *The Ring of the Nibelung* is scarcely surprising. But Wagner's anti-Semitism, as the account of his speech to Rubinstein suggests, was more than a bizarre peccadillo, beyond a prejudice: it was an obsession, a monomania, a full-blown neurosis. No conversation with Wagner ever occurred without a detour on the subject of Judaism. When, towards the end of Wagner's life, the painter Renoir had a sitting with him, Wagner interrupted his own pleasant flow of small talk with a sudden unprovoked denunciation of Jews which rapidly became rancid; after it subsided, he resumed the chit-chat. Sometimes the tone would be light and reasonable, but more often than not it would rapidly develop into hysteria.

And Wagner being Wagner it came with a huge apparatus of pseudo-science, pseudo-history and pseudo-psychology, much of it drawn from the toxic writings of the French racial theorist, Count Arthur de Gobineau, author of the pernicious *Essay on the Inequality of the Human Races*. Such was Wagner's admiration of the book that he befriended the good count. Indeed, Gobineau stayed with him in Bayreuth for the month preceding the rehearsals for *Parsifal*, a curious preparation for work on the nineteenth century's greatest expression of redemption, transcendence and forgiveness. A year earlier, Wagner told Cosima: 'if I were ever to write about the Jews again, I would say that I had nothing against them; the trouble is that they approached us Germans prematurely, when we were not sufficiently able to assimilate this element'. But it was untrue; to the end he was raging against Jews both in his salon and in the pages of his magazine *Bayreuther Blätter*, which was

edited by his acolyte, Hans von Wolzogen, a strident and virulent racist, who defined Wagner's life work as 'reforming the
world of the emotions along artistic lines' – code for de-Sem-
itisation. Wagner's last contribution but one to the paper was
as nauseatingly gung-ho anti-Judaic as ever. And even at the
dress rehearsal of *Parsifal*, as Levi made his way to the podium,
Wagner remarked to Cosima in his uniquely penetrating
voice, 'If I was an orchestral musician I'm not sure how I'd feel
about being conducted by a Jew.' This is a sort of madness.
Working on *Parsifal*, both Levi and Rubinstein preferred, they
said, to look for the man in his work, rather than his work in
the man. Wagner's son Siegfried thought that Rubinstein was
a kind of Kundry figure, yearning for redemption, which he
hoped to find through Wagner and his work, which is perfectly
possible: this is the kind of overheated relationship that many
people had with Wagner – 'the Master'.

The rehearsal period was infinitely calmer than that for *The
Ring*; it was, after all, only one opera rather than four. The
technical aspect was better managed, and Brandt's great
moving diorama – vast in dimensions – worked triumphantly;
the musical performance was astoundingly assured (thanks in
large part to Levi) and many of the singers penetrated to the
fathomless depths of their roles. Wagner was at last happy.
And it had been achieved, he said, 'by anarchy': everyone
doing just what he or she wanted to do, which happened to
be the right thing. Clearly everyone involved, he said, had
understood the entire undertaking and its purpose. The idea
of Bayreuth – the re-consecration of music-drama – had
triumphed. He had given *Parsifal* the unwieldy and almost
untranslatable designation of *Bühnenweihfestspiel* – stage festival dedication piece – to signal that he had taken the operatic
stage to an entirely new place, somewhere between religion
and theatre. This horrified some people and intoxicated
others. There were those who preferred to listen literally with

their eyes closed, separating the subject matter from the astonishing world of sound he had conjured, a translucent musical fabric constantly on the point of disintegration. It seemed to many of those first listeners to point to an unknown future for music. For Wagner, it was simply the achievement of his life's goal: he had translated the spirit of the Greek theatre into German form, rescuing German art and the art of the stage from the triviality and mediocrity which threatened to engulf both. It offered an antipode to life as it actually was: a world, he said, of 'murder and robbery, which were organised and legalised by lying, swindling and hypocrisy'. The opera draws on Christian imagery and myths, but it is not a Christian piece. It is, at its absolute core, a Schopenhauerian piece: it rejects the world as nothing but a tragic illusion. It offers no comfort, only the unearthly radiance that comes from acknowledgement of the unavoidable pain of existence.

There were seventeen performances. At the opening, there was none of the civic razzamatazz of the first festival. There were no emperors, no kings; not even Ludwig. Parzival did not attend his own opera. Musicians, especially young ones, flocked from all over Europe – Hugo Wolf, Mahler, Reger, Sibelius, Debussy. 'Incomparable and bewildering, splendid and strong,' wrote the Frenchman. '*Parsifal* is one of the loveliest monuments of sound ever raised to the serene glory of music.' But at the heart of the audience was that new phenomenon, the hard-core Wagner audience sometimes kitted out with Wotan hats and berets in homage to the Master: the faithful, irresistibly drawn to the sensual and emotional immersion that his work offered. It was a sort of drug, or a spell; exactly as he had planned, when they entered the Festspielhaus, people were tranced, taken to another world, their own inner world, to such an extent that they refrained from applauding, under the mistaken impression that it was what Wagner had decreed. When he shouted 'Bravo!' after the

Flower-Maidens' exit on the first performance, he was shushed by the rest of the audience. Afterwards, he complained that without hearing applause he didn't know how the piece had gone down. Lofty as his intentions were, Wagner was still, to his fingertips and to the very end, a man of the theatre.

At the last performance of the season, Wagner slipped unseen into the orchestra pit during Act III and took over from Levi for the opera's final scene, for the savage and terrible transformation music that brings the Grail Hall into view. Some of the knights carry in the coffined body of the just-deceased Grail King, Titurel; others bear the litter of Titurel's ailing son and heir, Amfortas. The furious knights hurl out stentorian protests at being denied sight of the Grail. Amfortas, racked with pain from his ever-bleeding wound, is desperately begging to be allowed to die:

> Come! You heroes!
> Slay now the sinner and end his woe,
> On you once more the grail then will glow!

Unnoticed, Parsifal appears in their midst; touching Amfortas with 'the wondrous, wounding holy spear', he heals him in an instant:

> O supreme joy of this miracle!
> This that could heal your wound
> I see pouring with holy blood
> yearning for that kindred fount
> which flows and wells within the Grail.
> No more shall it be hidden:
> uncover the Grail, open the shrine!

Parsifal mounts the altar steps, taking the Grail for the first time from the shrine opened by the squires, and falls to his knees in silent prayer and contemplation. The Grail gradually glows with a soft light; the darkness below intensifies, while the light above grows brighter and brighter.

> Miracle of supreme salvation!
> Our Redeemer redeemed!

A beam of light catches the Grail; it glows brighter than ever. From the dome a white dove descends and hovers over Parsifal's head. Kundry, relieved of the agony of her lust-torn existence, slowly sinks lifeless to the ground, her eyes lifted up to Parsifal; Gurnemanz and Amfortas, now healed, kneel in homage to him. He holds the Grail in blessing over the worshipping brotherhood of knights. The eighteenth-century Dresden Amen, which has constantly appeared during the opera – and which had figured in *The Ban on Love* and *Tannhäuser* – triumphs as the voices of the squires and the knights soar heavenward. When Wagner took over from Levi at the beginning of this ecstatic, unearthly sequence, the apotheosis of all the many redemptions in Wagner's work, he broadened the tempo hugely, challenging his singers' and his wind-players' lungs to breaking point. The expressive force of it was overwhelming, both to those on stage and to those in the auditorium. 'What that hour revealed to us,' wrote one of the audience, 'never came back.' Wagner himself stayed in the pit with the musicians, refusing to take a curtain call; he was in a mood of the greatest affability. He eventually made his way to the stage, and spoke to the artists and the company with such warmth that, according to Levi, they all dissolved into tears.

The festival had been a financial, an artistic and, for many, a spiritual success. Wagner and the family went back to Venice

yet again; they took the entire mezzanine floor of the magnificent Ca' Vendramin Calergi on the Grand Canal. Liszt joined
them there for eight weeks. Wagner started tinkering with
Tannhäuser all over again, hoping to clarify its meaning for
good and all. But there would be no new operas, he told
Cosima; now he would turn his attention to writing symphonies. Perhaps to put himself in a symphonic frame of mind, he
arranged, on Christmas Eve of 1882, as a birthday treat for
Cosima, a performance of the fresh-faced Symphony in C he
had written as a lad of nineteen. For the first time in many
decades, he had no project. He was in poor health, with stomach cramps and chest pains. Often he would sing to himself.
More than once, the family overheard him intoning the dead
Commendatore's terrible invitation from beyond the grave in
Don Giovanni: '*Don Giovanni a cenar teco m'invitasti e son
venuto!*' His thoughts turned again and again to death, here in
Venice. There were rumours of disease in the city; the perpetual blowing of the cool damp sirocco wind kept him at home,
though he made an exception so the children could see the
carnevale: he watched gloomily as the figure of Carnival was
carried to its grave to the accompaniment of the tacky old
tunes while the bells tolled midnight and all the brilliant
flares of the processions were suddenly extinguished across
the city. He felt, he told Cosima, like Othello, the Moor of
Venice: 'the long day's task is done'. He wondered whether she
still loved him: he knew how difficult he was. They lay in bed
one night, Cosima told her diary, 'and as I go to sleep, I hear
him speaking divine words to me, words I may not repeat,
words which wrap me around like guardian angels and settle
deep, deep in my heart like the most sacred of my treasures.
"Good night, my angel," I say. "Good night, my dear wife," he
replies. "That means so much more."'

He dreamed a great deal – of Schopenhauer, but also of
Wilhelmina Schröder-Devrient. 'All my women are now pass-

ing before my eyes.' He and Cosima read books out loud together, as they had always done. Wagner was especially taken by Fouqué's *Undine*, about a water nymph, 'the being who longed for a soul'. One afternoon, Cosima overheard him talking at the top of his voice. 'I was talking to you,' he said when she came in. Then he went over to the piano and played the music of those other briny creatures, the Rhinemaidens: their refrain, 'Rheingold, Rheingold', followed by their next phrase, 'False and base all those who dwell up above.' 'I feel loving towards them,' he told Cosima, 'these subservient creatures of the deep, with all their yearning.' That day, Levi, who had come to stay with them in Venice for a few days, took his leave. Wagner threw his arms round him, and showered him with kisses – the scion of a race he despised. Paradoxical to the last. The next day, 13 February, the sky was black with clouds, the rain torrential. Wagner, feeling unwell, retired to his room to work on his paper for the *Bayreuther Blätter*: 'The Feminine Element in Mankind'. 'The process of emancipation of the Woman,' he wrote, 'takes place amid ecstatic throes.' And then he wrote: 'Love – Tragedy.' In due course, the maid, Betty, heard him pacing rapidly up and down, then she heard him call her name; she ran for Cosima. 'I shall never forget the sight of my mother rushing out through our door,' wrote Siegfried Wagner. 'It expressed the force of the most passionate anguish; and she ran into the half-open door so hard it almost broke.' On his arrival, the doctor pronounced the composer dead.

'It is self-evident,' said the doctor's report, 'that the numerous psychical agitations to which Wagner was daily disposed by his peculiar mental constitution and disposition, his sharply defined attitude to a number of burning questions of art, science and politics, and his remarkable social life did much to hasten his unfortunate end.' In other words, Wagner died of being Wagner.

Cosima fell prostrate upon his lifeless body with a great cry and no persuasion could induce her to leave the corpse, which she continued to embrace for a whole day and night; then she cut off all her hair and placed it in the coffin. Neither food nor water passed her lips for four days. It appeared that she wanted to die.

She lived for another forty-seven years.

When Ludwig, now stout, toothless and doubtful of his own sanity, was told of Wagner's death, he stamped the floor so hard that the floorboard gave way. 'His corpse belongs to me,' he screamed. All the pianos in all his residences were draped in black crêpe thenceforth. Fifteen years earlier, he had told Sophie Charlotte that he would have a short life, linked as it was to the continued existence of Wagner. As he predicted, his star no longer shone, sundered from the remarkable, sweeping destiny of R. Wagner.

He lived for another three increasingly bewildered years after Wagner's death.

Hans von Bülow, who had suffered at Wagner's hands as much as anyone, fell into a profound depression. When he was told of the composer's death, all he was able to say – the words torn from him with great difficulty – was that 'he felt as if his soul had died with that fiery spirit, and that only a fragment of his body still wandered upon the earth'.

Nietzsche, on hearing of Wagner's death, misremembered how close they had been: 'like brothers', he said. When, six years later, he was admitted to the asylum at Jena, he told the doctors that 'it was my wife Cosima Wagner who brought me here'. He died in 1900, in the grip of howling insanity.

On hearing of Wagner's death, Verdi, Wagner's chief rival as an opera composer, wrote to his publisher, Giulio Ricordi: 'Sad, sad, sad. Wagner is dead. When I read the news yesterday I may truly say that I was completely crushed. Let us not discuss it. It is a great personality that has disappeared. A name which leaves a mighty imprint upon the history of art.' Verdi outlived Wagner, his exact contemporary, by 18 years, during which time he wrote his masterpieces, *Otello* and *Falstaff*.

CODA

Wagner's coffin was solemnly conveyed by gondola to the Venice railway station and thence by train to Bayreuth, where it was interred in the garden at Wahnfried, in the tomb which he had made sure was completed at the same time as the house, so that he could spend time in it. The path through the garden to the vault was his favourite walk. Sometimes he invited other people to join him there, while he discoursed on death and dying. 'Ah, I wish I was already in it!' was his frequent cry. Death had been his constant companion for over twenty years. The stupendous achievements of those years had been a result of willpower – nothing else. He had lived, in the words of Faust he chose for the epigraph to his overture on the subject, with the feeling that:

> the hell that is inside me sends
> terrible dreams to fill my head.
> Deep in my soul, God stirs the springs,
> but cannot move external things.
> Existence is become a mere, dead weight:
> Would death could free me from the life I hate.

Wahnfried was rapidly converted by Cosima into a hero's mausoleum. The restless, unsettling, destructive, sublime, dynamic spirit of Richard Wagner turned to stone. But what he wrote cannot be confined. It remains as restless, unsettling, destructive, sublime and dynamic as it ever was. He is everywhere. Music was changed utterly by him, in the work both of those who followed the path he opened up – Mahler, Strauss, Schönberg – and those, like Debussy and Stravinsky, who redefined themselves to escape his influence. He transformed opera. He revolutionised theatre. He entered the collective unconscious of twentieth-century literature in the work of Claudel and Yeats and Pound and Eliot; Thomas Mann, appalled and fascinated by him in equal measure, confronted him head on again and again, above all in his great lecture 'The Sufferings and Greatness of Richard Wagner', which, in 1933, earned him thirteen years' exile from Germany.

After Wagner's death, his creation, Bayreuth, was stopped in its tracks by Cosima, who tried to preserve it exactly as he had left it; it catered to the faithful, for whom attending his works was a religious experience, more Lourdes than Epidaurus. This is scarcely what Wagner had intended. In time, Wagner's son, Siegfried, homosexual and liberal, took over from his mother and attempted to distance Bayreuth from some of his father's positions, notably his anti-Semitism: 'whether a person is a Chinese, a Negro, an American, a Red Indian or a Jew, is a matter of complete indifference to us', he wrote to a racial purist who had complained at the presence of Jews in the audience. But Siegfried was dead by 1930, and the wife he had been forced to marry to escape scandal grasped the helm. Winifred Wagner, English-born and single-minded, threw in her lot with the now irresistibly rising Nazi party, forming an intensely close relationship with the man she called 'Wolf'. Hitler had been a fervent Wagnerian from his youth in Vienna, when he had been overwhelmed by *Rienzi*. As Winifred Wagner told the film-maker Jürgen Syberberg, he extended his personal protection to Bayreuth, which included waiving the strict racial laws, with the result that even during the war, Jewish singers and players received special dispensations to perform there. As it happens, Hitler's enthusiasm for Wagner was shared by few of his associates; he tried to impose his passion on the party, but it didn't work. After the Nuremberg rally, he made a block booking for *The Mastersingers of Nuremberg* at Bayreuth, filling the theatre with party members. Ensconced in the stalls, they quickly got bored, fell asleep, or talked amongst themselves; at the interval they drank themselves into a stupor. In a fit of pique, the Führer cancelled all further party visits to Bayreuth. But the rank and file's boredom and boorishness were the least of the problem: the more intellectually acute of the high command pointed out that *The Ring of the Nibelung* was a proto-Marxist text, and that *Parsifal* was dangerously close to a religious experience, which was equally repugnant to the Nazi ethos. In fact, *Parsifal* was banned during the war years. But performances of Wagner's music in extract – in concerts, especially and most prominently those conducted by Wilhelm Furtwängler with the Berlin Philharmonic – were identified throughout the free world as synonymous with the Nazi regime, especially since the Allies had cleverly appropriated Beethoven's Fifth Symphony for their own purposes.

When the Allies took Germany in the summer of 1945, the Wagner family was unceremoniously turfed out and the Festspielhaus turned, with brutal symbolism, into an entertainment venue; the only opera performed in the theatre built to accommodate *The Ring* and *Parsifal* was *Die Fledermaus*. Just five years later, as part of the general reconstruction of post-war Germany, Bayreuth and Wagner were rehabilitated. Winifred's sons Wieland and Wolfgang were installed as artistic directors, though their mother was banned in perpetuity from even entering the building; to the end of her enormously long life, she insisted that Hitler had been a dear, good, misunderstood man. With her out of the way, something astonishing happened at Bayreuth in that first post-war season: Wieland, the elder of the brothers, had spent the war working in a non-military capacity at the nearby Institute for

Physical Research, and used the facilities available to him to construct set models and experiment with lighting, as he pondered how to progress the staging of his grandfather's work. His first post-war production – of *The Ring of the Nibelung* – jettisoned the entire Nordic and Teutonic imagery Bayreuth had so long cultivated, shifting decisively away from either historicism or realism. The stage picture was of the utmost simplicity, greatly dependent on light and the expressive physical movement created by Wieland's wife, the dancer and choreographer Gertrud Reissinger; in Patrick Carnegy's vivid phrase, he pioneered the 'opera as mystery play', thus bringing the work infinitely closer to the composer's vision. Many people detected a Jungian dimension to Wieland's approach, an engagement with archetypes and a universal symbology. It was radical not only in terms of staging Wagner's work, but for the theatre generally. Halfway through the twentieth century, Wagner was again at the forefront of the avant-garde.

The operas continued to stimulate a huge variety of interpretations wherever and whenever they were performed. After Wieland's early demise, Wolfgang assumed sole and highly autocratic control of Bayreuth, but continued to invite provocative directors to stage productions there; Bayreuth was never safe, artistically. The family meanwhile fell into vicious in-fighting, which finally resolved itself with the appointment of Wolfgang's two daughters (from different wives) as co-directors of the festival. But this appointment too turned savage, with Katharina before long banning her half-sister from attending rehearsals. The Wagnerian dimension of all this, with rival siblings and half-siblings and a patriarch losing control, was lost on no one; but under Katharina's sole command, Bayreuth has evolved to a startling degree into a forum in which Germany could confront its past – which is not exactly what Wagner had in mind, but it was, in another sense, exactly what he wanted: music drama at the centre of society.

Before Freud and Jung, Wagner made the old myths mean something again; like them, he looked beyond the rational brain. He saw man as a turbulent, troubled, writhing, longing, betraying, creating, destroying, loving, loathing mess of instincts and impulses so deeply buried within us that we scarcely dare look at them. He forced us to do so. He was all of these things himself. Had he been anything other than a musical genius, he would have been locked up.

He cannot bring comfort.

Which is why people fight over him, why they always have done and why they always will do, now and forever. He upsets people because that is precisely what he set out to do. Despite the fact that the moment a *Ring* cycle is announced it sells out, whatever the price of tickets (usually inordinate) – despite 5,000 people a night choosing to swelter, spellbound, through concert performances of the operas at the BBC Proms in London, with twenty times that number clinging to their radios to listen to it at home and even more watching worldwide on television – there are still people who do not simply dislike his music, they find it intolerable, unendurable, offensive. His music is banned, for goodness' sake. We understand why. But his capacity for upsetting people long pre-dates its association with the Nazis (whom he would have despised, loathing as he did both militarism and imperialism). Wagner is like the wolf he once tried to tame – he cannot be house-trained. As long as what we call classical music exists, Wagner will be performed, but he will never be a classic, comfortably installed in the pantheon. He is a whirlpool at the centre of musical culture, dangerous and dynamic. He is the discomfort we must live with, taking us perhaps reluctantly away from the songs of sun-infused Apollo and towards the darker, differently blissful turmoil of Dionysus. Only a truly uncommon human being could have been the conduit for this work. Anyone less extraordinary would have been destroyed by it. But he rode the dragon with skill and guile and tenacity, while lesser men would have been thrown at the first canter. We should be grateful, even if we may be glad that we don't have to spend too much time in his company.

CHRONOLOGY

1813   22 May: Richard Wagner born in Leipzig. 23
       November: death of father, Carl Friedrich Wagner.
1821   30 September: Ludwig Geyer, Richard's stepfather,
       dies.
1822   Attends school in Dresden, as Wilhelm Richard Geyer.
1825   Performs Weber's *Der Freischütz* for friends.
1826   Translates first three books of Homer's *Odyssey* into
       German.
1827   Begins *Leubald: a Tragedy*. Drops the name Geyer.
1828   Studies at the Nikolai-Gymnasium.
1829   Sees Wilhelmine Schröder-Devrient perform on stage,
       and decides to become a musician. Composes piano
       sonatas, string quartet.
1830   Arranges Beethoven's Ninth Symphony for piano.
       Composes three overtures, including the *Drum Beat*,
       which is performed in Leipzig.
1831   Studies music with Theodor Weinlig.
1832   Works on *The Wedding*. Symphony in C performed in
       Prague. Piano Sonata in B-flat major published.
1833   Composition of *The Fairies*.
1834   Musical director in Lauchstädt and Magdeburg.
       Beginning of relationship with Minna Planer.
1835   Works on *The Ban on Love*.
1836   Premiere of *The Ban on Love*. 24 November: marries
       Minna Planer.
1837   Appointed musical director in Riga. Rosalie Wagner
       dies.

1838 Begins work on *Rienzi*.

1839 Flight from Riga. Wagner escapes his creditors. Travels to London and then to Paris.

1840 Completes *Rienzi*. First version of *Faust* overture. Meets Liszt.

1841 Composition of *The Flying Dutchman*.

1842 Richard and Minna leave Paris for Dresden. 20 October: premiere of *Rienzi* in Dresden.

1843 2 January: premiere of *The Flying Dutchman* in Dresden. Takes on the position of Court Kapellmeister in Dresden. Composes *The Apostles' Love Feast*.

1844 Works on *Tannhäuser*. *The Flying Dutchman* opens in Berlin, *Rienzi* in Hamburg. Weber's remains brought to Dresden from London.

1845 19 October: premiere of *Tannhäuser* in Dresden. Prose sketches of *The Mastersingers of Nuremberg* and *Lohengrin*.

1846 Begins composition of *Lohengrin*. Conducts Beethoven's Ninth Symphony for the first time.

1848 9 January: death of Wagner's mother, Johanna. Wagner gets involved in politics and becomes a revolutionary. Prose sketch for *The Ring of the Nibelung*. Libretto-poem for *Siegfried's Death*.

1850 Exile in Zurich. Writes *Judaism in Music*. 28 August: premiere of *Lohengrin* in Weimar, under direction of Franz Liszt.

1851 Writes *Opera and Drama*.

1852 Completes libretto-poem of *The Ring of the Nibelung* in Zurich.

1853 Composes Prelude to *The Rhinegold*. Concerts in Zurich. Writes piano sonata for Mathilde Wesendonck.

1854 Reads Schopenhauer's *The World as Will and Presentation* for the first time. First ideas for *Tristan and Isolde*.

1855 Revises *Faust* overture. Travels to London where he gives eight concerts.

1856 23 March: completion of *The Valkyrie*. First sketches for *Siegfried*.

1857 Stays at the Wesendoncks'. Relationship between Richard and Minna deteriorates. 9 August: completes sketches to Act II of *Siegfried*. Writes libretto and begins composition of *Tristan and Isolde*.

1858 The relationship between Richard and Mathilde Wesendonck causes a separation between Richard and Minna. Minna goes to Dresden. Wagner leaves for Venice, where he works on *Tristan*.

1859 Completes *Tristan and Isolde*. Travels to Paris, where Minna joins him.

1860 Conducts his own music in Paris. Partial amnesty from German Confederation.

1861 *Tannhäuser* in Paris. Sees *Lohengrin* for the first time, in Vienna, where rehearsals for *Tristan* begin. Reads libretto of *The Mastersingers of Nuremberg* to friends.

1862 Last meeting with Minna, in Biebrich. Works on *The Mastersingers of Nuremberg*. Conducts *Lohengrin* for the first time (in Frankfurt). Spends time with Minna in Dresden, the last time they see each other. Full amnesty from Saxon king.

1863 Concert tours in Austria, Czechoslovakia, Hungary, Russia. Wagner and Cosima von Bülow meet in Berlin, and declare that they belong to each other.

1864 In flight from creditors. King Ludwig II invites Wagner to Munich; Wagner moves into Haus Pellet by Lake Starnberg. Cosima and Hans von Bülow stay with him for two months. Wagner conducts first Munich performance of *The Flying Dutchman*.

1865 10 April: birth of Isolde, first child of Richard and Cosima. Premiere of *Tristan and Isolde* in Munich.

Wagner begins writing *My Life*. Completes Act II of *Siegfried*. 10 December: Wagner is driven out of Bavaria.

1866 25 January: death of Minna Wagner. Wagner settles in Tribschen, near Lucerne. Works on *The Mastersingers of Nuremberg*.

1867 Cosima in Tribschen. 17 February: Eva, second child of Richard and Cosima, born. Cosima finally leaves Bülow. *Mastersingers* completed.

1868 21 June: premiere of *Mastersingers* in Munich. Wagner and Nietzsche meet in Leipzig. Cosima moves in with Wagner in Tribschen permanently.

1869 Nietzsche starts visiting Tribschen on a regular basis. Wagner begins Act III of *Siegfried*. Birth of Siegfried Wagner. Premiere of *The Rhinegold* in Munich; Wagner not present. Starts work on *The Twilight of the Gods*.

1870 Premiere of *The Valkyrie* in Munich; Wagner absent. Official divorce of Cosima and Hans von Bülow. Wagner and Cosima marry in Lucerne. 25 December (Cosima's birthday): first performance of *Siegfried Idyll*.

1871 Completion of *Siegfried*. Wagner chooses Bayreuth as location for his festival.

1872 Moves to Bayreuth. Foundation stone is laid for the construction of the Festspielhaus. Tours Germany with Cosima recruiting performers for the first season.

1873 Reads libretto of *The Twilight of the Gods* to friends and patrons in Berlin. Gives concerts in Hamburg, Cologne and Berlin.

1875 Extensive concert tours in Vienna, Budapest and Berlin. Further rehearsals in Bayreuth. Wagner directs productions of *Tannhäuser* and *Lohengrin* in Vienna.

1876 Wagner writes *Grand Festival March in Celebration of the American Declaration of Independence*. *Tristan and*

Isolde in Vienna to raise funds for Bayreuth. August: first Bayreuth Festival opens with *The Ring of the Nibelung*: three complete cycles performed. Wagner and family travel to Italy. Meets Nietzsche one last time in Sorrento.

1877 First American performance of *The Flying Dutchman*, in New York. Wagner begins working on *Parsifal*. Concerts in London and for Queen Victoria at Windsor. Reads *Parsifal* libretto to friends in Heidelberg.

1878 Wagner conducts Prelude to *Parsifal* at Villa Wahnfried. Continues working on the opera.

1879 More work on *Parsifal*. Second festival postponed again.

1880 Works on *Parsifal* during ten-month Italian sojourn. Conducts Prelude to *Parsifal* in Munich for Ludwig; they never meet again.

1881 Another long sojourn in Italy, working on *Parsifal*. Frequently ill.

1882 January: *Parsifal* at last completed, in Palermo, Sicily. Rehearsals in Bayreuth, under the baton of Hermann Levi. After the festival, Wagner travels to Venice with family. Conducts his early Symphony in C in Teatro La Fenice.

1883 Starts pamphlet on 'The Feminine Element in Mankind'. 13 February: Wagner dies in Venice. 18 February: funeral in Bayreuth.

WAGNER'S WORKS

From John Deathridge, Martin Geck, and Egon Voss's *Wagner Werk-Verzeichnis (WWV): Verzeichnis der musikalischen Werke Richard Wagners und ihrer Quellen* (Schott Musik International, Mainz, London, & New York, 1986). I have translated the German opera and titles into English.

1	tragedy	*Leubald* (1826–28)
2	piano	Sonata in D minor
3	aria	Aria (1829; lost)
4	chamber music	String Quartet in D major
5	piano	Sonata in F minor
6	opera	*Pastoral Opera* (*Lovers' Caprices*) (early 1830?; lost)
7	*lieder*	Lieder (1828–30; drafts)
8	aria	Aria for soprano and orchestra (early 1830?; lost)
9	arrangement	Piano reduction of Ludwig van Beethoven's Symphony No. 9 in D minor, Op. 125 (1830–31)
10	orchestral	Overture in B-flat major (*Drum-Beat*) (1830; lost)
11	orchestral	*Political Overture* (*c.*1830; lost)
12	orchestral	Overture to Schiller's *The Bride of Messina* (1830; lost?)
13	orchestral	Fragment of an orchestral work in E minor (*c.*1830)
14	orchestral	Overture in C major (1830; lost)

15	*lieder*	Seven Compositions on Goethe's *Faust*
16	piano 4-hands	Sonata in B-flat major, for four hands
17	orchestral	Overture in E-flat major (1831; lost)
18	arrangement	Piano reduction of Haydn's Symphony No. 103 in E-flat major (1831; lost)
19A	choral	Study fugue *Thine is the Kingdom* (1831–32)
19B	choral ?	Double Fugue (1831–32)
20	orchestral	Concert Overture No. 1 in D minor (1831)
21	piano	Sonata in B-flat major, Op. 1 (1831)
22	piano	Fantasia in F-sharp minor (1831)
23A	piano	Polonaise for piano (1831–32)
23B	piano 4-hands	Polonaise for piano, four hands (1832)
24	orchestral	Overture in E minor and Theatre Music to Raupach's *König Enzio*
25	orchestral	*Entracte tragique* No. 1 in D major (fragment)
26	piano	Grand Sonata in A major (1832)
27	orchestral	Concert Overture No. 2 in C major
28	aria	Scene and aria for soprano and orchestra
29	orchestral	Symphony in C major
30	*lieder*	*Evening Bells*
31	opera	*The Wedding* (1832–33)
32	grand romantic opera	*The Fairies*
33	aria	Aria No. 15 (Aubry) *Like a Lovely Spring Morning* from the opera *The Vampire* by Heinrich Marschner with

		a new allegro 'But now, wherever I look, I am confronted by horrors of the night'
34	arrangement	Instrumentation of a cavatina from Bellini's *The Pirate*
35	orchestral	Symphony in E major
36	orchestral	Music for the *Pageant for the Arrival of the New Year 1835*
37	orchestral	Overture to Guido Theodor Apel's historic drama *Columbus*
38	grand comic opera	*The Ban on Love or The Novice of Palermo*
39	orchestral	*Polonia* (Wagner); Overture in C major
40	grand opera	*The Noble Bride*
41	incidental music	Music for the play *The Last Heathen Conspiracy in Prussia or The German Knightly Order in Königsberg* by J. Singer, Sketches
42	orchestral	*Rule Britannia*. Overture in D major
43	aria	*'Gentle melancholy longs to stir'*. Aria for bass and orchestra. Excerpt from the opera *Mary, Max und Michel* by Carl Blum
44	choral	Folk hymn *Nicolay*
45	aria	Bass aria from *The Swiss Family*
46B	arrangement	Giacomo Meyerbeer: *Robert Le Diable* No. 18 (C). Cavatina and re-orchestration
46C	arrangement	Carl Maria von Weber: *Euryanthe* No. 18. Hunting chorus and re-orchestration
46D	arrangement	Fromental Halévy: *The Guitarist* for several instruments

46E	arrangement	Arrangements of Halévy's *The Queen of Cyprus*
46F	arrangement	Daniel Auber: *Zanetta or Playing with Fire*. Arrangement for flute and string trio, Suites No. 1 and 2
47	arrangement	Gioachino Rossini: *Les soirées musicales*, No. 12 Duet 'Li Marinari', instrumentation
48	comic opera	*Man's Wit trumps Woman's*, or *The Happy Bear Family*
49	grand tragic opera	*Rienzi, the Last of the Tribunes*
50	*lieder*	*The Christmas Tree*
51	choral	Funeral music for Julies von Holtei
52	choral ?	*Norma, il predisse, o Druidi*, aria for bass, male chorus, and orchestra from the opera *Norma* by Vincenzo Bellini
53	song	*Dors mon enfant*
54	song	*Extase* (fragment)
55	song	*Attente*
56	song	*La tombe dit à rose* (fragment)
57	song	*Mignonne*
58	song	*Tout n'est qu'images fugitives* (Soupir)
59	orchestral	*Faust Symphonie*, first movement (*A Faust Overture*, first version)
59	orchestral	*Faust Overture* (second version)
60	song	*Les deux grenadiers*
61	song	*Adieux de Marie Stuart*
62B	arrangement	Arrangements from Gaetano Donizetti's opera *La favorite*
62C	arrangement	Henri Herz: *Grande Fantaisie sur La Romanesca fameux air de danse du XVI siècle*, Op. 111. Arrangement for piano four-hands

62E	arrangement	Arrangements of Fromental Halévy's opera in five acts *The Queen of Cyprus*
63	romantic opera	*The Flying Dutchman* (1840–1841)
64	piano	*Album Leaf for Ernst Benedikt Kietz: Song without Words*
65	piano ?	*'Descendons gaiement la courtille'.* Contribution to the Vaudeville-Ballet-Pantomime *La descente de la courtille* by Th. Marion Dumersan and Ch.-Désiré Dupeuty, for chorus and orchestra
66	opera	*The Saracen Woman*
67	opera	*The Falun Mine*
68	choral	Cantata *The Day Breaks*
68A	choral	*Cantata on the Unveiling of the Monument to Friedrich Augustus*
69	choral	*The Apostles' Pentecost*
70	grand romantic opera	*Tannhäuser and the Song Contest on the Wartburg* (1842–45)
71	choral	*Greeting from his Loyal People to Friedrich August* (II of Saxony)
72	choral	*At Weber's Grave*
73	orchestral	Funeral music
74	arrangement	Orchestration of Spontini's *La vestale*
75	romantic opera	*Lohengrin* (1850)
76	opera ?	*Friedrich I*
77	arrangement	Arrangement of Christoph Willibald Gluck's tragic opera *Iphigénie en Aulide*
78	orchestral	Symphonies
79	arrangement	Giovanni Pierluigi da Palestrina: *Stabat mater*; arrangement
80	opera	*Jesus of Nazareth* (1849; scenario and 1 musical sketch)

81	opera ?	*Achilleus* (1849–50)
82	heroic opera	*Wieland the Smith* (1849–50; scenario only)
83	arrangement	Arrangement of Mozart's *Don Giovanni* (1850)
84	piano	*Polka* (1853)
85	piano	*A Sonata for the Album of Frau MW* (1853)
86A	Stage Festival Play, preliminary evening	*Das Rheingold* (1853–54)
86B	Stage Festival Play, first day	*Die Walküre* (1854–56)
86C	Stage Festival Play, second day	*Siegfried* (1856–71)
86D	Stage Festival Play, third day	*The Twilight of the Gods* (1869–74)
87	arrangement	Concert ending for the Overture to Gluck's *Iphigenie in Aulis* (1854)
88	piano	*Zurich Sweetheart-Waltzes* (1854)
89	opera	*The Victors* (1856; 1878)
90	drama	*Tristan and Isolde* (1857–59)
91	*lieder*	*Wesendonck Lieder* (1857–58)
91B	orchestral	*Dreams* from *Wesendonck Lieder* (1857)
92	*lieder*	*It is Surely God's Will* (c.1858; draft)
93	orchestral	*Romeo and Julie* (1868; sketches)
94	piano	*In Princess M's Album*
95	piano	*Arrival at the Black Swan*
96	opera	*The Mastersingers of Nuremberg* (1845–67)

97	orchestral	*Homage March*. Arrangement for military music (1864 Cuvilliés Theatre)
98	orchestral ?	*So-called Themes*
99	opera	*Luther's Wedding* (1868; prose sketches)
100	comedy	*A Comedy in One Act* (1868)
101	choral	*A Slogan for the German Fire Brigade* (1869)
102	comedy in the old style	*A Capitulation* (1870)
103	orchestral	*Siegfried Idyll* (1870)
104	orchestral	*Emperor March* (1871)
105	*lieder*	*Minor Songs* (1871)
106	*lieder* ?	*Child's Catechism for Kosel's Birthday* (1873)
107	*lieder* ?	*So-called Themes* (1874–83)
108	piano	*Album Leaf for Frau Betty Schott* (1875)
109	arrangement	Arrangement of the Waltz *Wine, Women and Song* by Johann Strauss II (1875)
110	orchestral	*Grand Festive March for the Opening of the Centennial Celebration of the Signing of the Declaration of Independence of the United States of America* (1876)
111	Festival Play for the Consecration of the Stage	*Parsifal* (1877–82)
112	*lieder*	*Minor Songs* (1877)
113	*lieder*	*Minor Songs* (1880)

Reproduced by permission of SCHOTT MUSIC, Mainz, Germany

BIBLIOGRAPHY

These are prominent among the many, many books I have consulted, but they represent a tiny fraction of what has been and is being written on the subject:

Amerongen, Martin Van, *Wagner: A Casebook Study*, Dent, 1983

Borchmeyer, Dieter, *Drama and the World of Richard Wagner*, Princeton University Press, 2003

Carnegy, Patrick, *Wagner and the Art of the Theatre*, Yale University Press, 2006

Deathridge, John, *Wagner: Beyond Good and Evil*, University of California Press, 2008

—and Dahlhaus, Carl, *The New Grove Wagner*, Macmillan, 1984

DiGaetani, John Louis, *Wagner and the Modern British Novel*, Farleigh Dickinson University Press, 1978

Goldman, Albert, and Sprinchorn, Evert, *Wagner on Music and Drama*, Gollancz, 1964

Hurn, Phillip Dutton, and Root, Waverley Lewis, *The Truth about Wagner*, Cassell, 1930

Köhler, Joachim, *Nietzsche and Wagner: A Lesson in Subjugation*, Yale University Press, 1998

—*Richard Wagner, The Last of the Titans*, trans. Stewart Spencer, Yale University Press, 2004

Lippert, Woldemar, *Wagner in Exile*, trans. Paul England, Harrap, 1930

McIntosh, Christopher, *The Swan King: Ludwig II of Bavaria*, Tauris, 2003

Magee, Bryan, *Aspects of Wagner*, Alan Ross, 1968
—*Wagner and Philosophy*, Allen Lane, 2000
Millington, Barry, *The Sorcerer of Bayreuth: Richard Wagner, His Work and His World*, Oxford University Press, 2012
Neumann, Angelo, *Personal Recollections of Wagner*, trans. Edith Livermore, Constable, 1909
Newman, Ernest, *A Study of Wagner*, Dobell, 1899
—*Wagner as Man and Artist*, Dent, 1914
—*The Life of Richard Wagner*, Cassell, 1945
Praeger, Ferdinand, *Wagner as I Knew Him*, Longman, Green, 1892
Rose, Paul Lawrence, *Wagner: Race and Revolution*, Faber, 1992
Sabor, Rudolph, *The Real Wagner*, André Deutsch, 1989
—*Wagner Celebration*, International Press, 2004
Skelton, Geoffrey, *Richard and Cosima Wagner: Biography of a Marriage*, Gollancz, 1982
Spencer, Stewart, *Wagner Remembered*, Faber and Faber, 2000
Spotts, Frederic, *Bayreuth: A History of the Wagner Festival*, Yale University Press, 1994
Tanner, Michael, *Nietzsche*, Oxford Paperbacks, 1994
—*Wagner*, HarperCollins, 1996
Williams, Simon, *Wagner and the Romantic Hero*, Cambridge University Press, 2004

Some of the best and most stimulating recent writing on Wagner is to be found in essay collections, among which *Penetrating Wagner's Ring*, edited by John Louis DiGaetani (Da Capo), is, despite its hilarious title, one of the best. *Richard Wagner and His World*, edited by Thomas S. Grey (Princeton) and *The Wagner Handbook*, edited by Müller and Wapnewski (Harvard), are both full of excellent and provocative contributions, while Paul Dawson-Bowling's two-volume *The Wagner Experience and Its Meaning to Us* (Old Street) is a unique production, the work of a passionate and curious Wagnerite who has devoted himself to a lifelong quest for the ultimate truths of the composer's life and work.

Wagner's own writings are readily available, in a variety of editions and translations. The bulk of them can still only be found in the ponderous and cumbersome versions of Wagner's first translator, William Ashton Ellis, to whom non-German speakers must nonetheless be grateful; Dodo Press has also done us all a great service by bringing them out in cheap, attractive paperback editions. All Wagner's major and many of the minor writings are to be found in the Dodo catalogue. Very few of these pieces, pamphlets and books are available in modern or even relatively modern versions. In 1970, Albert Goldman and Evert Sprinchorn brought out a very useful digest of Wagner's prose writings, with highly illuminating commentaries, under the title *Wagner on Music and Drama* (Gollancz); the texts themselves, alas, are drawn from the Ashton Ellis translations. A scintillating compilation of the young Wagner's stories, essays and articles, edited and translated by Robert Jacobs and Geoffrey Skelton under the title *Wagner Writes from Paris* (Allen and Unwin), gives a sense of how engaging a writer he could be. Skelton was also responsible for the indispensable abridged translation of *Cosima Wagner's Diaries*. The most vivid sense of Wagner's personality is to be discovered in his letters, of which a vast quantity is now available, largely, alas, rendered into dreary English by the indefatigable, if verbally tone-deaf Ashton Ellis. They appear scattered across countless collections – *Family Letters; Letters to Theodor Uhlig; Letters to August Röckel; Letters to Minna; Letters to Liszt* (both of these last two bursting with life) – many of them available from Dodo Press, or Print on Demand. Fortunately, in their *Selected Letters* (Dent), Stewart Spencer and Barry Millington made a deeply stimulating choice which gives a sense not only of what was going on inside Wagner's head, but also of his day-to-day experience. Finally, and perhaps most usefully of all, in 1983 Cambridge University Press published a sparkling and vivid new translation of *My Life* by Andrew Gray, edited by Mary Whittall, an edition which, with its invaluable notes and comprehensive afterword describing the background of the book, its errors and prevarications, is a crucial item in any reading of Wagner, and should be as widely and easily available as possible if this extraordinary man is to be understood.

As a kind of pendant to Wagner studies, Nietzsche's writings about Wagner are evidence of a reaction to the man and his music that many listeners have experienced on a less titanic scale. The books in which he writes about Wagner, all readily available in excellent translations, are:

The Birth of Tragedy
Untimely Meditations: Richard Wagner at Bayreuth
The Case of Wagner
Nietzsche contra Wagner

The following works have been quoted in translation:

Goethe, Johann Wolfgang von, *Faust: Parts 1 and 2*, trans. Robert David MacDonald, Oberon, 1988

Hoffmann, E. T. A., 'Review of Beethoven's Fifth Symphony', in David Charlton (ed.), *E. T. A. Hoffmann's Musical Writings*, trans. Martyn Clarke, Cambridge University Press, 1989

— *The Life and Opinions of the Tomcat Murr*, trans. Anthea Bell, Penguin, 1999

Schopenhauer, Arthur, *The World as Will and Presentation Vol. 2*, trans. Richard Aquila and David Carus, Prentice Hall, 2011

ILLUSTRATIONS

All illustrations, except the portrait of Wagner by Joukowsky (p. 180), are taken from Kreowski and Fuchs, *Richard Wagner in der Karikatur*, B. Behr's Verlag, Berlin, 1907.

ACKNOWLEDGEMENTS

First to thank is Kasper Holten, without whom none of this would have happened. Then Simon Stokes and Robin Don, my collaborators on *Inside Wagner's Head*, who waited with infinite patience till I found what it was I wanted to say about Wagner. Then Professor Bryan Magee, in addition to writing two of the very best books on the subject – the pithy and provocative *Aspects of Wagner*, and then, thirty years later, the magisterial *Wagner and Philosophy* – spent some priceless time with me, helping me to clarify my understanding of the way Wagner's mind worked. Any lucidity the book may have in the territory of philosophy is due to these conversations.

Next to thank is the late George Weidenfeld, who had the idea for a book, but who, perhaps more importantly, by offering a pair of his tickets for Bayreuth to my friend Andrew Paulson, who in turn invited me to see *Tristan and Isolde*, *Parsifal* and *The Mastersingers of Nuremberg*, opened my eyes to the whole idea of Wagner as a phenomenon, rather than simply a musician. Then I must thank Martin Redfern for so eagerly and swiftly responding to my proposal for a book, and Arabella Pike for taking it forward with such enthusiasm, then Kate Johnson and Lottie Fyfe who combed the manuscript for solecisms, orthographic, grammatical, factual, and stylistic and patiently put up with my spirited defences of some deeply ingrained idiosyncrasies. Then, as ever, I must thank Maggie Hanbury, my agent, for her endless informed encouragement and for making it all happen smoothly and to the book's best advantage. Renaissance man and supreme maestro of the keyboard Stephen Hough read the book in a slightly earlier form, and made shrewd and penetrating comments on it, all of which have been absorbed into the present version. Composer, musicologist, educator, writer, Gerard McBurney and I have discussed Wagner over many years, and his kaleidoscopically brilliant mind has thrown shaft of light after shaft of light onto aspects of the composer's approach which were otherwise opaque to me; these illuminations too have found their way into the text.

Finally, my husband Sebastian has endured nearly four years of exposure to my astonished discoveries and barely formed ideas about a composer with whom we have lived in the sort of intellectual ménage-à-trois of which I suspect *der Meister* would have fully approved.

INDEX